AF335665

The Power® Of:
SMART SOFTWARE SYSTEM

by

Robert E. Williams

Edited

by

Estelle M. Phillips

Management Information Source, Inc.

...anagement Information Source, Inc.
1107 N.W. 14th Avenue
Portland, Oregon 97209
(503) 222-2399

First Printing

ISBN 0-943518-59-8

The Smart Software System is a product of
Innnovative Software, Inc.
P.O. Box 25372
Overland Park, Kansas 66210
(913) 345-2424

The Power Of:[T.M.] is a registered trademark of Management
Information Source, Inc.

**ONE OF A SERIES OF INSTRUCTIONAL MANUALS ON
THE USE AND APPLICATION OF COMPUTER MANUALS**

INTRODUCTION

The Power Of: Smart Software System is a book designed for users of the Smart Software program who have little or no experience using a computer. The instructions guide users, step-by-step, one keystroke at a time, through specific application samples, enabling them to rapidly gain the ability to utilize this powerful program and apply the knowledge to their own personal needs.

The Time-Manager exercise teaches how to set up a calendar of appointments, which includes descriptions of meetings and tasks. The printing of various types of calendar reports is demonstrated.

The Word Processing exercises teach the fundamentals of the program, as well as the creation of a macro, the combining of two word processing documents, and the merging of a word processing document with a graph and a database.

The Spreadsheet exercises demonstrate the setting up of Cost Recovery, Amortization Schedule and Budget Consolidation spreadsheets.

The Database exercises teach how to create a database and use many of Smart Software's database functions, such as entering a formula which performs mathematical calculations on particular database fields. The merging and printing of a mailing list with a form letter is also demonstrated.

The Smart Software System includes the Smart Communications Program. Its powerful features were not covered in this book, so for details on its operation refer to the Smart System Manual. The Smart Communications Program performs two major functions. It is a terminal emulation program allowing you to dial another computer system and act as a terminal, and it is a file transfer program. This allows the exchange of files between two computer systems. Among the many features of the Smart Communications Program are "Quick Keys" for selecting communications commands and performing special tasks, and the program's capability of emulating a standard ANSI

terminal. Projects that perform unattended communications
can easily be created using the project processing
capabilitites available throughout The Smart System. For
example, a project could be created which would
automatically place a call to another office in a distant city,
during nighttime hours (when telephone rates are low), for
the purpose of retrieving important information, and then
print a series of reports which will be ready and waiting
early the following morning.

Business owners, secretaries, journalists, accountants,
attorneys, manufacturers, engineers, scientists, architects,
educators, students, or anyone using a personal computer,
will find The Power Of: Smart Software System a valuable
companion to the Smart Software program.

**IF YOU OWN OR ARE THINKING OF OWNING SMART
SOFTWARE SYSTEM, YOU SHOULD OWN THIS BOOK!**

ACKNOWLEDGEMENT

A special thank you is given to Stan Christ,
Suzanne Beveridge and Dave Coburn, along
with other members of the Innovative
Software, Inc., staff, for their help in solving
particular problems relating to the writing of
this book. Their patience and generous
attitude are much appreciated by the staff of
Management Information Source, Inc.

Estelle M. Phillips,
Senior Editor

TABLE OF CONTENTS

(continued)

i

EXERCISE FIVE

Merges a word processing form letter with a
database of names and addresses, and prints out
merged information.

EXERCISE SIX

Determines investment balance still owing on a
purchased item. Updating procedure is detailed.
Profit being made and total number of months item
has been in service is calculated.

EXERCISE SEVEN

Uses program's Pmt and Principal functions to
calculate unknown payment or principal of a loan.
Generates report containing principal, principal
payment, interest payment, principal to date, and
interest to date for the length of the term.

EXERCISE EIGHT

The exercise create three worksheets: the first
for budget information on Office 1; the second for
information on Office 2; the third for
consolidating the data of the two offices, to
obtain an overall view of a company's budget.

EXERCISE NINE

Teaches the fundamentals of the program's database
facility. Details creation of a customized screen,
entering of data, and the calculation of running
totals. The use of a formula to calculate
particular fields is shown. Updating, deleting and
purging of records is demonstrated, as well as the
use of Browse, GoTo and Find commands. Printing of
records, selected fields, and records in list
format is detailed.

INDEXES

EXERCISE 1
TIME-MANAGER

DESCRIPTION

Smart System provides a Time-Manager program which enables you to schedule business and personal appointments.

After information is entered regarding dates, type of appointments, descriptions, etc., the program can display a calendar for the entire month, or just the week.

Short or long reports can be printed out for the day, week or month information.

In this exercise you will set up and print two reports. The first one will be a complete report and will include the entire month's entries. The second will be a shorter version of the same report.

OPERATIONS PERFORMED

Creating a Filename

Entering Information

Displaying Weekly and Monthly Schedules

Assigning Tasks and Giving Priorities

Entering Information for Another Meeting

Assigning Tasks and Giving Priorities

Printing a List of Meetings, Tasks and Priorities

Deleting a Meeting

Using the GoTo Command

Exiting Smart Time Manager

COMMANDS USED

DISPLAY
FIND
GOTO
INSERT
LOAD
OUTPUT
PURGE

HOW TO ACCESS THE TIME MANAGER PROGRAM

NOTE

Before proceeding with this exercise, you *must* place a
blank formatted data diskette into Drive B.

Carefully follow the directions below.

After you have loaded the Smart System Disk into your
computer, a list of the available programs is displayed.
Press:

T   selects Time-Manager option

The following message is displayed:

Place Time-Manager diskette in drive, enter any key

NOTE

There is no Time-Manager diskette. The Time
Manager program is on the Smart Communications
diskette.

Remove the Smart System Disk and replace it with the
<u>SMART COMMUNICATIONS</u> disk. Press:

RETURN   loads Time-Manager program onto
                          the screen

CREATING A FILENAME

When Time Manager is displayed on your screen, you will see
two boxes on the top half of the screen. The one on the left
is for Meetings; on the right for Tasks. The area at the
bottom is for descriptions.

At the bottom of the screen, Command List 1 is displayed,
listing the various commands.

Before entering information you must first create a filename,
using the LOAD command, onto which the program can save
your work as you proceed. Press:

L	starts LOAD command and displays: Enter time file name:
July	filename Note: name must not exceed 8 characters, and cannot contain spaces
RETURN	displays: July does not exist, create it (y/n)
Y	Yes, to create the file

Observe that, at the bottom of your screen, in the center,
File: july is now displayed.

ENTERING INFORMATION

To begin entering information, press:

I	starts INSERT command
M	selects Meeting option and displays Meeting Parameters:

The date on the computer's system clock will be displayed.

Leave your cursor where it is and type:

07-05-85	date for meeting
RETURN	enters date and moves cursor to Time:

Type:

09:30am	time
RETURN	enters time and moves cursor to Short Description:

Type:

Convention	text to be entered
RETURN	displays Edit Description:

After reading the following note, type in the description as illustrated below.

NOTE

After typing the word **presented**, DO NOT TYPE the word RETURN. Just *press* RETURN and continue typing.

Now type:

This meeting is for the purpose of organizing the displays to be presented [RETURN] at the next computer convention to be held in Boston, Oct. 5-8, 1985.

After the description is typed in, press:

F10 function key
records the entry and displays Command List 1

At this point, there will be no change visible on your screen. (The computer system date will still be displayed.)

DISPLAYING WEEKLY AND MONTHLY SCHEDULES

You will now use Time-Manager's Week and Month options to see a weekly and monthly calendar of the information you have just entered.

First you must FIND the information to be displayed. Press:

F   starts FIND command

F   selects First option and displays
                                information on screen

Your screen should appear similar to the Figure 1 below.

07-05-85 Friday

--Meetings--   --Tasks--

9:30am Convention

This meeting is for the purpose of organizing the
displays to be presented at the next computer
convention to be held in Boston, Oct. 5-8, 1985.

Figure 1

To view the week screen, press:

D   selects DISPLAY command
                           and displays options

W   selects Week option
                           and displays a calendar for the week of
                           June 30, 1985

Observe that the specified day for the meeting, Fri 5, is
highlighted, and that a small diamond symbol is displayed in
the 9 am row.

To view the month screen, press:

Esc   displays Command List 1

D   starts DISPLAY command

M   selects Month option and displays
                           a calendar for the month of July 1985

Observe that the date you specified for the meeting, July 5,
is highlighted. Press:

Esc   displays Command List 1

ASSIGNING TASKS AND GIVING PRIORITIES

You will now enter information for the meeting regarding
particular tasks to be performed, and you will give a priority
to each task. Press:

I   starts INSERT command

T   selects Task option and displays
                           Task Parameters:

RETURN   moves cursor to Priority:

1   indicates that first priority
is to be given to the task

RETURN   moves cursor to Short Description:

Leave the cursor where it is and type:

Decide on theme.   text to be entered

RETURN   displays Edit Description

Read the next note and then type in the following text.

NOTE

After you type the word **and,** DO NOT TYPE the
word RETURN. Just *press* RETURN to move the
cursor down to the next line.

**A decision has to be made as to the thrust of the poster
advertising, and [RETURN] how many areas should be
covered.**

When you are finished, press:

F10 function key
                     displays information on screen in Task
box, with description of task in area
below.

To enter another task, press:

I   starts INSERT command

T   selects Task option and displays
Task Parameters

RETURN   moves cursor to Priority:

2   indicates that 2nd priority is
to be given to the following task

RETURN   moves cursor to Short Description:

Type:

Select graphics people.

RETURN   displays Edit Description:

Type in the following text:

There is a question concerning the advisability of using the same graphics [RETURN] arts people again. The validity of certain complaints have to be [RETURN] considered.

Press:

F10 function key
          displays second task with appropriate description below

To enter another task, press:

I   starts INSERT command

T   selects Task option and displays Task Parameters

RETURN   moves cursor to Priority:

3   indicates that 3rd priority is to be given to the following task

RETURN   moves cursor to Short Description:

Type:

Decide on # of posters.

RETURN   displays Edit Description:

Type in the following text:

Each booth at the convention must have at least one poster; some need two. [RETURN] Decide on total number, after ascertaining amount needed for mailing.

Press:

F10 function key
          displays third task on screen, with
          appropriate description below

ENTERING INFORMATION FOR ANOTHER MEETING

There is another important meeting to be scheduled for July. To enter the information on your calendar, press:

I
          starts INSERT command

M
          selects Meeting option
          and displays Meeting Parameters:

Type:

07-18-85
          date for meeting

RETURN
          enters date and moves cursor
          to Time:

Type:

08:00am
          time to be entered

RETURN
          enters time and moves cursor
          to Short Description:

Type:

Travel
          text to be entered

RETURN
          displays Edit Description

Type in the description as illustrated below.

**Travel arrangements have to be made well in advance for the
sales [RETURN] representatives. Because of the Frustrata
Airline strike, alternative [RETURN] travel arrangements
must be discussed.**

After the description is typed in, press:

F10 function key

        displays Command List 1

To view the meeting information just entered, in Week form,
you must first locate it. Press:

F	starts FIND command
L	selects Last option and displays information on screen
D	selects DISPLAY command and displays Select Option: Week Month
W	selects Week option and displays a calendar for the week of July 14, 85.

Observe that the specified meeting date, Thursday, July 18,
is highlighted, and a diamond shaped indicator is displayed
in the 8 am row.

To view the meeting in Month form, press:

Esc	displays Command List 1
D	starts DISPLAY command
M	selects Month option and displays a calendar for the month of July 1985
Esc	displays Command List 1

ASSIGNING TASKS AND GIVING PRIORITIES

Now you will enter two tasks for the second meeting, and assign priorities to them.

I   starts INSERT command

T   selects Task option
and displays Task Parameters:

RETURN   moves cursor to Priority:

2   indicates that second
priority is to be given to the task

RETURN   moves cursor to Short Description:

Type:

Contact airlines.

RETURN   displays Edit Description:

Type in the following text.

Make reservations on another airline, in case the strike continues.

When you are finished, press:

F10 function key

displays information in Task box at
right half of screen.

To enter another task, to which you will assign top priority, press:

I   starts INSERT command

T   selects Task option and
displays Task Parameters

RETURN   moves cursor to Priority:

1
        indicates that 1st priority is
to be given to the following task

RETURN
        moves cursor to Short Description:

Type:

Verify itinerary.

RETURN
        displays Edit Description:

You wish to have this area left blank, so you can pencil in comments at the meeting, so type nothing here. Press:

F10 function key
        displays first priority task on screen, without accompanying description.

Observe that the second priority Task has automatically moved down to make room for the first priority Task.

PRINTING A LIST OF MEETINGS, TASKS AND PRIORITIES

Now you will utilize the OUTPUT command to print a list of all meetings and tasks. The meetings are printed out in chronological order; tasks are printed out according to their priority.

In this exercise, you will print out both a long and a short list. The long list is illustrated in Figure 2; the short list in Figure 3.

To print a long list for the entire month, press:

O
        starts OUTPUT command

M
        selects Month option

L   selects Long option and prints
                               a long version of all meetings for month
                               of July

Your printout should look like Figure 2.

Observe that in the report for July 18, there is a blank area
underneath **Priority 1...Verify itinerary,** which is useful for
jotting down handwritten notes during a meeting.

Next you will print a short version of the July meetings.

O   starts OUTPUT command

M   selects Month option

S   selects Short option
                               and prints a short version
                               of all meetings for month of July

Your printout should look like Figure 3.

To print a long or short report for just one *week*, use the
FIND command to locate the week to be printed, and then
use the OUTPUT command, and select the Week option,
either short or long.

To print a long or short report for just one *day*, use the
FIND command to locate the day to be printed, and then use
the OUTPUT command, and select the Day option, either
short or long.

DELETING A MEETING

The PURGE command is used for deleting a day, week or
month from the calendar.

Now you will use the PURGE command to *permanently* delete
a meeting and its tasks.

```
                        JULY  5, 1985 FRIDAY
                        --------------------


  Priority: 1 ....... Decide on theme.
  -------------------------------------------------------------------------
  : A decision has to be made as to the thrust of the poster advertising, and :
  : how many areas should be covered.                                          :
  :                                                                            :
  -------------------------------------------------------------------------


  Priority: 2 ....... Select graphics people.
  -------------------------------------------------------------------------
  : There is a question concerning the advisability of using the same graphics :
  : arts people again. The validity of certain complaints have to be           :
  : considered.                                                                :
  -------------------------------------------------------------------------


  Priority: 3 ....... Decide on # of posters.
  -------------------------------------------------------------------------
  : Each booth at the convention must have at least one poster; some need two. :
  : Decide on total number, after ascertaining amount needed for mailing.      :
  :                                                                            :
  -------------------------------------------------------------------------


  Time: 9:30 Am ..... Convention
  -------------------------------------------------------------------------
  : This meeting is for the purpose of organizing the displays to be presented :
  : at the next computer convention to be held in Boston, Oct. 5-8, 1985.      :
  :                                                                            :
  -------------------------------------------------------------------------
```


```
                        JULY 18, 1985 THURSDAY
                        ----------------------


  Priority: 1 ....... Verify itinerary.
  -------------------------------------------------------------------------
  :                                                                            :
  :                                                                            :
  :                                                                            :
  -------------------------------------------------------------------------


  Priority: 2 ....... Contact airlines.
  -------------------------------------------------------------------------
  : Make reservations on another airline, in case the strike continues.        :
  :                                                                            :
  :                                                                            :
  -------------------------------------------------------------------------


  Time: 8:00 Am ..... Travel
  -------------------------------------------------------------------------
  : Travel arrangements have to be made well in advance for the sales          :
  : representatives. Because of the Frustrata Airline strike, alternative      :
  : travel arrangements must be discussed.                                     :
  -------------------------------------------------------------------------
```

Figure 2

```
                              JULY  5, 1985 FRIDAY
                              ----------------------

   Priority: 1 ....... Decide on theme.

   Priority: 2 ....... Select graphics people.

   Priority: 3 ....... Decide on # of posters.

   Time: 9:30 Am ..... Convention
```

```
                              JULY 18, 1985 THURSDAY
                              ----------------------

   Priority: 1 ....... Verify itinerary.

   Priority: 2 ....... Contact airlines.

   Time: 8:00 Am ..... Travel
```

Figure 3

First you must GOTO the meeting to be deleted. Press:

G   starts GOTO command and displays
                          Date:

Type:

07-05-85   date to go to

RETURN   displays information
                          for 07-05-85

P   starts PURGE command

D   selects Day option and
                          permanently deletes information for
                          July 5, 1985

USING THE GOTO COMMAND

You just used the GOTO command to go to a particular date.

You can use the GOTO command to move forward or
backward any number of days you wish.

The date at the top of the screen now is July 5, 1985. Press:

G   starts GOTO command and displays
                          Date:

Type:

45   number of days to go forward

RETURN   moves forward 45 days
                          and displays 08-19-85 Monday

To go backward in the year's calendar, press:

G   starts GOTO command
                                and displays Date:

Type:

-90   number of days to go backward
                                Note: To move backward, you *must* type
                                a minus sign before the number of days.

RETURN   moves backward 90 days and
                                displays 05-21-85 Tuesday

To move forward an entire year, press:

G   starts GOTO command and displays
                                Date:

365   number of days to go forward

RETURN   moves forward a year and
                                displays 05-21-86

EXITING SMART TIME MANAGER

To exit Time Manager, press:

F10 function key
                                saves work and displays Select option:

Q   selects Quit option and
                                displays:
                                Save changes made to July (y/n)

Y   Yes, saves changes
                                and exits program

EXERCISE 2
CREATING A WORD PROCESSING DOCUMENT
AND A MACRO

DESCRIPTION

In this exercise you will make a series of changes in a
business letter, including the insertion, deletion and
replacement of text.

Boldfacing and indenting of text will also be demonstrated.

A Smart Word Processor macro will be created and used to
quickly insert text. Finally the document with the macro will
be saved, and a parameter will be set for future automatic
loading of the macro.

OPERATIONS PERFORMED

Using the Entry and Command Modes

Naming the Document

Typing the Document

Inserting Characters

Deleting Characters (Two Methods)

Typing Over Text

Inserting Additional Words Into the Text

Inserting Blank Lines

Replacing Text

Indenting Text

Placing Indented Text Back on Left Margin

Boldfacing

Creating a Macro

Saving a Macro

Setting Parameter for Automatic Loading of Macro

Saving the Document

Printing the Document

Clearing the Screen

Loading a Document

COMMANDS USED

BOLD
LOAD
MACRO
NEWNAME
PARAMETERS
PRINT
REPLACE
SAVE
UNLOAD
VISIBLE

Before typing the letter which is illustrated in Figure 1, read
the following information, and then follow the instructions
for typing the letter.

USING THE ENTRY AND COMMAND MODES

When Smart Word Processor is first loaded into your
computer, a blank screen is displayed for entering text. You
are in Text Entry mode, which means you can begin entering
text.

At the bottom of the screen are the quick-keys. To access the
Commands, press the Escape key. To return to Text Entry
mode and and quick-keys, press Escape again. The escape key
acts as a toggle switch, enabling you to switch back and
forth between Entry mode and Command mode.

Cursor Key Position

When the program is first displayed on your screen, the
cursor location is indicated by a blinking underscore (_).
However, if the character insertion mode parameter is set to
Insert OFF, the program displays a half-height cursor.

Insert ON mode

The blinking underscore (_) also means that the Insert mode
is turned on, and you will see the words **Insert ON** displayed
at the lower right hand corner of your screen. This means
that whatever you type will be inserted into the text.

The Insert mode can be turned off by pressing the Ins
(Insert) key. Then text that you type will be typed OVER
current text. When the Insert mode is turned off, the words
Insert OFF will be displayed at the lower right hand corner
of your screen, and the blinking underscore takes on the
appearance of a blinking *square*.

NOTE

A ruler is displayed at the bottom of your screen . The
symbol **L** on the ruler indicates the position of your left
margin. The **R** indicates the position of the right margin.

Wordwrap

The Smart Word Processor knows when you have reached the
end of a line and provides an automatic carriage return. The
only time you need to press the RETURN key is at the end
of a paragraph, or where formatting requires it.

Cursor Key Movement

The cursor keys are located on the right-hand side of your keyboard.

The up arrow cursor key, located on number 8, moves the cursor up one line.

The down arrow cursor key, located on number 2, moves the cursor down one line.

The right arrow cursor key, located on number 6, moves the cursor to the right one character.

The left arrow cursor key, located on number 4, moves the cursor to the left one character.

NAMING THE DOCUMENT

Now you are ready to create a business letter.

The first operation is to name the document you will be typing. If you do not see the Commands displayed, press:

Esc   displays Command List 1

3   displays Command List 3

N   starts NEWNAME command

Bowyer   filename for document

RETURN   names the document and
                        displays: **Document: bowyer** on the status
                        line, at the bottom left-hand side of the
                        screen

TYPING THE DOCUMENT

Now that the document has been named, you are ready to type in the document which is illustrated in Figure 1.

To return to Enter Mode, press the Escape key.

Type:

Travel Reservations

RETURN   moves cursor to Line 2

Observe that, at the end of Line 1, a symbol is displayed which represents the RETURN you entered.

To make the symbol invisible, press:

Esc 2   displays Command List 2

V   starts VISIBLE command

P   selects Paragraph-Marks
                         option and eliminates the display of
                         RETURN symbols in your document

Also observe that the diamond shaped symbol, which indicates the end of the document, has also been made invisible.

Esc   returns to Edit mode

Continue typing in the document illustrated in Figure 1, pressing RETURN only where indicated in Figure 1.

NOTE

We have deliberately put misspelled words into the document, so type it exactly as illustrated. If you make mistakes while typing, you will be shown how to correct them later.

```
Travel Reservations  [RETURN]
Attn: Joan Boyer, Agent  [RETURN] [RETURN]

Dear Ms Bowyer:  [RETURN] [RETURN]

As  a  result  of our recent  telephone  conversation,  I  am
forwarding this lQletter to confirQm first-class seating  for
Mr.  Arnold Rubin,  Promotions Director,  Housatonic Millwork
Company,  aboard  SAS flight 838 leaving Boston  for  warsaw,
.Tuesday,  July 03, and returning to Boston, Sunday,  November
05.  [RETURN] [RETURN]

·Mr.  Rubin's entire itinerary has now been completed,  and  I
would  appreciate it if you would arrange first-class  ground
transportation  and  hotel accommodations  at  the  following
locations.  [RETURN] [RETURN]

London:  July 22-25  [RETURN]
Stockholm:  September 1-19  [RETURN]
Oslo:  October 15-24  [RETURN] [RETURN]

Any late or additional changes in this schedule will be  made
after Mr.  Rubin arrives in Europe.  His transactions will be
concluded  through  the  use  of  a  VISA  charge  card,  No.
892-295-33700.  [RETURN] [RETURN]

Please  provide complete details including hotel  and  ground
transportation  rates at the locations mentioned  above.   If
there  is  any additional information I can  provide,  please
feel free to contact me.  [RETURN] [RETURN]

Sincerely,  [RETURN] [RETURN] [RETURN]


Hazel Woodward, Curator  [RETURN]
```

Figure 1

When the document has been typed in, hold down the Control
key and press the Home key. This places your cursor at the
top of the document.

INSERTING CHARACTERS

There is a w missing in the name **Boyer** on Line 2. To insert
the letter in the proper place, first be sure that Insert ON is
displayed at the bottom right-hand corner of your screen.

Using the arrow cursor keys, place your cursor on the y in
Boyer on Line 2, and type:

w   inserts w, and moves the
                        text to the right

DELETING CHARACTERS (TWO METHODS)

The word **lQletter** on Line 7 is misspelled. The l and **Q** must
be deleted.

Using your arrow cursor keys, place your cursor on the *first*
letter (the l) in **lQletter** on Line 7 and press:

Del Del   Delete key, deletes the
                   character the cursor is on

If you continue to press the Delete key, you will be able to
delete additional characters to the right of the cursor.

The word **confirQm** on Line 7 is also misspelled.

Here you will try another method of deletion.

Place your cursor on the **m** in **confirQm**, and press:

Backspace key   deletes the character
                   to the left of the cursor

If you continue to press the Backspace key, you will be able
to delete additional characters to the left of the cursor.

TYPING OVER TEXT

You will note that the w in **warsaw** on Line 9 needs to be capitalized.

Before you can type over a character, you need to turn the Insert mode off. Press:

Ins

Insert key, turns Insert
mode off
Note: The words Insert ON
at the lower right hand corner of the
screen now read: Insert OFF

Observe that the status line at the bottom of your screen displays Ln:7, which indicates the line your cursor is presently on.

Place your cursor on Line 9 and observe the status line as you move down. When you reach Line 9, you will see Ln:9 displayed.

Place your cursor on the *first* w in **warsaw** on Line 9, and hold down the Shift key and press **W**.

To return to the Insert On mode, press:

Ins

Insert key, turns Insert
Mode ON

The Insert key acts as a toggle switch, enabling you to switch back and forth between Insert ON and Insert OFF.

INSERTING ADDITIONAL WORDS INTO THE TEXT

You now find it necessary to insert some additional words in Line 13.

Place your cursor on the space following the word itinerary on Line 13 and type:

, from London to Stockholm,

As you type, you will observe the wordwrap function
automatically moves the text to the right of the insertion,
but the text needs reformatting. Press the down cursor key
once to reformat.

INSERTING BLANK LINES

The itinerary would stand out better if it were spaced
differently.

Place your cursor on the space at the end of Line 18 and
press:

RETURN   inserts a blank line

Place your cursor on the space at the end of Line 20 and
press RETURN to insert a blank line.

REPLACING TEXT

You have decided to replace the word **ground**, which appears
on Lines 15 and 29, with the word **automotive**.

Hold down the Ctrl key and press Home key to get to top of
the document. Press:

Esc 1   displays Command List 1

R   starts REPLACE command
                      and displays: Enter search text:

ground   text to look for

RETURN   displays Enter
                      Replacement text

automotive   replacement text

RETURN   displays options

G   selects Global option

RETURN   replaces the two occurrences of
                               ground with the word automotive

NOTE

The Replace options allow the program to look
forward or backward for text.

Use the G (Global) option if you don't know the exact
location of the text to be replaced, or if you wish all
occurrences of a portion of text to be replaced. and
the program will search the entire document
regardless of cursor position.

The C (Conditional) option will prompt you for
confirmation of each replacement, instead of
replacing automatically.

The I (Ignore case) option searches for text without
regard to upper and lower case.

W (Whole word) option searches for a match that is
preceded and followed by a space. Use this option
when searching for small words like "the" "at" or "of",
so the program will find the exact word, instead of
finding words that merely contain those letters, as
"amphitheatre, create or sofa.

INDENTING TEXT

The first line of the document should be indented.

Hold down the Ctrl key and press the Home key.

Leave your cursor on the **T** in **Travel** on Line 1 and press:

Esc   returns to Edit mode

Tab Tab Tab Tab   indents the heading

PLACING INDENTED TEXT BACK ON LEFT MARGIN

If you wish to place the heading back at the left margin,
hold down the Control key and press:

Home   places cursor on first
                        Tab symbol, on Line 1

Del Del Del Del   moves heading back to left
                        margin

Now, for this exercise, indent the heading again by pressing
Tab 4 times.

BOLDFACING

The itinerary would have a more pleasing appearance if it
were displayed in boldface typeface. Press:

Esc 2   displays Command List 2

Place your cursor on the L, the first character on Line 18.
Press:

B   starts BOLD command

I   selects INSERT command

B   selects Block option

Press:

F2 function key (drop anchor)

Move your cursor to Line 22 and place it on the 4, the last
character on Line 22.

RETURN   boldfaces the block of text

NOTE

> If you are using a standard text monitor or graphics
> monitor in the graphics display mode, the boldfacing
> will be visible on your screen.

When the text is printed out, it will appear in boldface
typeface.

CREATING A MACRO

Macros can easily be created by utilizing the SMART WORD
PROCESSOR'S Macro command.

A macro is a series of keystrokes which are recorded by the
program and assigned a key. Whenever that particular series
of keystrokes is needed, all you have to do is type the
assigned key symbol for the macro, and the program will
automatically perform the recorded keystrokes for you.

For example, you find that you frequently want to enter, at
the bottom of a letter, information to expedite filing.

The letter you just typed will be filed under Historical
Society. You will create a macro which will automatically
enter that phrase in italics typeface, with a single keystroke.

Leave your cursor on any location and press:

5	displays Command List 5
M	starts MACRO command
D	selects Define option
*	asterisk, the key which will be assigned to the macro Note: Type the asterisk, by holding down the Shift key and pressing the number 8 on the top row of your keyboard.

Next you will create the macro. Press:

F6 function key

                    displays **F6**, which
                    means Select Font

1

                    the number **1**, which
                    selects the Italics option

Now press:

RETURN

                    displays **Cr**, which means
                    Carriage Return

Now type:

Historical Society

Now press:

F6 function key

                    displays **F6**, which
                    means Select Font

Type:

0

                    zero, for standard font

RETURN

                    displays **Cr**, which
                    means Carriage Return

Last, press:

F10 function key

                    records the macro

Esc

                    returns to Enter mode

To try out the macro, first go to the bottom of the document
by holding down the Control key and pressing:

End

                    End key, moves cursor
                    to end of document

Press the RETURN key three times to insert 3 blank lines.

To execute the macro,

Hold down the Shift key and press:

*   asterisk, key assigned to the macro

Observe that the words Historical Society have been inserted at the cursor position, and are in italics typeface.

Anytime you wish to use the macro to insert the phrase, access the asterisk (*) by holding down the Shift key and pressing the number 8 on the top row of your keyboard.

SAVING A MACRO

To save your macro, press:

Esc 5   displays Command List 5

M   starts MACRO command

S   selects Save option
                      and displays Enter macro filename:

HS   filename

RETURN   saves the macro

SETTING PARAMETER FOR AUTOMATIC LOADING OF MACRO

To set the parameter for automatic loading of the macro file, press:

P   starts PARAMETERS command
                               and displays Word Processor Parameters
                               on screen

Press the down cursor key until the arrow indicator is
pointing to Automatic load of macro file, and type:

hs
                        the name of
                        the macro to be loaded automatically

F10 function key
                        ends process

SAVING THE DOCUMENT

To save your document with the macro, press:

4   displays Command List 4

S   starts SAVE command
                        and displays Enter filename:

RETURN   saves the file

PRINTING THE DOCUMENT

To print the letter, press:

1   displays Command List 1

P   selects PRINT command

N   selects Normal option

bowyer   filename

RETURN   displays options

P   selects Printer option and displays
         Enter number of copies:

RETURN   automatically selects one copy
         and displays Enter start page
         number:

RETURN   automatically starts with first
         page and prints document

Your document should look like Figure 2.

CLEARING THE SCREEN

To clear your screen, press:

4   displays Command List 4

U   starts UNLOAD command
         and clears screen

LOADING A DOCUMENT

To see how the macro works, press:

L   starts LOAD command

Bowyer   filename to load

RETURN   loads the file

Now place your cursor on any blank line, and press:

Esc   returns to Entry mode

Hold down the Shift key and press:

*   asterisk, macro to be
         executed

The phrase Historical Society should appear automatically.

```
                    Travel Reservations
Attn: Joan Bowyer, Agent

Dear Ms Bowyer:

As  a  result  of our recent  telephone  conversation,  I  am
forwarding this letter to confirm first-class seating for Mr.
Arnold  Rubin,   Promotions  Director,   Housatonic  Millwork
Company,   aboard  SAS flight 838 leaving Boston  for  Warsaw,
Tuesday,   July 03, and returning to Boston, Sunday,  November
05.

Mr.  Rubin's entire itinerary, from London to Stockholm,  has
now  been completed,  and I would appreciate it if you  would
arrange  first-class  automotive  transportation  and  hotel
accommodations at the following locations.

London:  July 22-25

Stockholm:  September 1-19

Oslo:  October 15-24

Any late or additional changes in this schedule will be  made
after Mr.  Rubin arrives in Europe.  His transactions will be
concluded  through  the  use  of  a  VISA  charge  card,  No.
892-295-33700.

Please   provide   complete  details  including  hotel   and
automotive  transportation rates at the  locations  mentioned
above.  If there is any additional information I can provide,
please feel free to contact me.

Sincerely,


Hazel Woodward, Curator



Historical Society
```

Figure 2

EXERCISE 3
COMBINING TWO WORD PROCESSING DOCUMENTS

DESCRIPTION

In this exercise Smart Word Processor's COPY and INSERT commands will be used to combine two word processing documents.

First a book list will be created containing information that requires frequent updating. Next a standard paragraph, containing information which seldom requires change, will be created.

The standard paragraph will be copied to Smart Word Processor's copy buffer, stored there, and then inserted into the book list document.

In this exercise, only one standard paragraph will be inserted into text. However, in lengthy documents where repetition of standard paragraphs is frequently required, Smart Word Processor's COPY and INSERT procedure will be appreciated. The program allows you to create as many "standard paragraphs" as you wish and then insert the paragraph(s) into any portion of a document as often as you wish.

Margin width adjustment, tab clearing and setting, and centering of text, will also be demonstrated in this exercise, as well as making paragraph, return and tab symbols invisible.

OPERATIONS PERFORMED

Making Paragraph And Return Symbols Invisible

Adjusting Margin Width

Removing All Tab Settings

Setting A New Tab

COMMANDS

COPY
INSERT
JUSTIFY
LOAD
MARGIN
PRINT
REPLACE
SAVE
TABS
UNDERSCORE
UNLOAD
VISIBLE

MAKING PARAGRAPH AND RETURN SYMBOLS INVISIBLE

After the Smart Word Processor program has been loaded into your computer, a diamond symbol is displayed at the upper left of the screen, indicating end of document.

To make the diamond symbol, and future paragraph marks, invisible, press:

Esc   displays Command List 1

2   displays Command List 2

V   starts VISIBLE command

P   selects Paragraph-Marks option
                           and makes the diamond symbol
                           invisible, as well as future paragraph
                           marks

ADJUSTING MARGIN WIDTH

Before typing the book list document, the right margin needs to be widened. Command list 2 is already displayed, so press:

M   starts MARGIN command

R   selects Right option

The message: **Enter new right margin, or use Tab or cursor keys to move to column:**

Press the right arrow cursor until the message reads:

Enter new right margin, or use Tab or cursor keys to move to column: 75

RETURN   enters new Right margin and
                           displays Command list 2

Observe that the R on the ruler has moved to the right.

REMOVING ALL TAB SETTINGS

The next step, before typing the book list, is to remove all the tab settings. Command List 2 is still displayed on the screen, so press:

T   starts TABS command

N   selects Normal option

Observe the ruler at the bottom of the screen. A blinking cursor is now positioned on the letter L. (The L represents Left margin)

Press the F6 function key *seven* times, so that the blinking cursor is on the R. (The R indicates the Right margin)

To clear all tab settings, press:

F9 function key   clears all settings

SETTING A NEW TAB

A new tab must now be set.

Press the F5 function key twice, which moves the blinking cursor back to the horizontal line following the number 5, and press:

F3 function key   sets new tab

Press:

F10 function key   finishes procedure and
                             displays Command list 2

TYPING THE BOOK LIST

You are now ready to *use the following directions* for typing in the document (the book list) which is illustrated in Figure 1.

The title should be centered. *Before* typing it in, press:

J   starts JUSTIFY command

C   selects Centered option
                           and moves cursor to center of screen

Esc   returns to Text-Entry mode

Now you are ready to type in the title.

Press the Caps Lock key once to turn it on.

Type the following, keeping it all on one line:

SCHEDULE OF READINGS FOR THE GREAT BOOKS DISCUSSION CLUB

Press the Caps Lock key once to turn it off, and press:

RETURN RETURN moves cursor down to Line 3

Observe that the cursor is still in the center of the document. The document must be formatted back to normal jusification. Press:

Esc   displays Command List 2

J   starts JUSTIFY command

N   selects Normal option
                           and places cursor back at left margin

Esc   returns to Text-Entry mode

```
          SCHEDULE OF READINGS FOR THE GREAT BOOKS DISCUSSION CLUB

Text:                                               Author:

January readings:

The Loneliness of the Long Distance Runner         Sillitoe

The Visit to the Museum                            Nabakov

February readings:

The Tempest  (Act One)                             Shakespeare

Heart of Darkness                                  Conrad

March readings:

Death in Venice                                    Mann

The World as Will and Idea                         Schopenhauer
```

Figure 1

To continue typing the letter, type:

Text:

Press the Tab key once. Your cursor is now located at the
new tab setting. Type:

Author:

RETURN RETURN moves cursor down to Line 5

MAKING TAB SYMBOLS INVISIBLE

Observe the symbol following the word **Text:**. This is a tab
symbol. To make this symbol invisible, press:

Esc   displays Command list 2

V   starts VISIBLE command

T   selects Tabs option and makes the
                          Tab symbol, and all future Tab symbols,
                          invisible

Press:

Esc   returns to Text-Entry mode.

Type:

January readings:

NOTE

Do not attempt to do any underlining at this point.
Underlining will be detailed in the next paragraph of
this exercise.

RETURN RETURN moves cursor down to Line 7

Type:

The Loneliness of the Long Distance Runner

Press the Tab key once. Type:

Sillitoe

RETURN RETURN moves cursor down to Line 9

Continue typing in the book list as illustrated in Figure 1, remembering to utilize the new tab setting to reach the Author column.

When you have finished typing the book list, right after typing the word **Schopenhauer,** press:

RETURN RETURN   moves cursor down to Line 23

UNDERLINING TEXT

The appearance of the book list would be enhanced if certain phrases were underlined. Press:

PgUp key   move up one screen

Place your cursor on the **J** in **January** on Line 5, and press:

Esc   displays Command list 2

U   starts UNDERSCORE command

I   selects Insert option

L   selects Line option and underlines
                            the text on Line 5

Next place your cursor on Line 11 (anywhere in the phrase **February readings:**) and press:

U   starts UNDERSCORE command

I   selects Insert option

L   selects Line option

The phrase **February readings:** is now underlined.

Place your cursor on Line 17 (anywhere in the phrase March **readings:)** and press:

U   starts UNDERSCORE command

I   selects Insert option

L   selects Line option

The phrase **March readings:** is now underlined.

Your screen should look like Figure 1.

SAVING THE BOOK LIST

To save the document, press:

4   displays Command list 4

S   starts SAVE command

booklist   filename

RETURN   saves the document

TYPING THE STANDARD PARAGRAPH

The next operation is to type the standard paragraph which will be inserted into the book list.

First unload the booklist. Press:

U   starts UNLOAD command and clears
                           the screen

Esc   returns to Text-Entry mode

Next type in the paragraph which is illustrated in Figure 2
below.

```
Book  lovers  of  all ages are welcome  at  the  GREAT  BOOKS
DISCUSSION CLUB meetings.    All that is required is that  you
read the selection to be discussed.  Meetings are held at the
home  of Mr.  and Mrs. Henri Phillips,  101  Kerchel  Street,
Lakewood,  Ohio,  at  7:30  p.m.,  on  the  first  and  third
Wednesdays  of every month.  For further information  on  the
reading selections, call Mae or Henri Phillips at 555-1234.
```

Figure 2

When you are finished typing the paragraph, press:

RETURN   moves cursor to Line 8.

Press:

Home   Home key, places cursor at the
                          upper left hand corner of the text, on
                          the B in Book.

SAVING THE STANDARD PARAGRAPH

Now save the standard paragraph. Press:

Esc 4   displays Command list 4

S   starts SAVE command

stdpara   filename

RETURN   saves

STORING THE STANDARD PARAGRAPH IN THE COPY BUFFER

The next operation is to store the standard paragraph in the program's Copy buffer. Press:

1   displays Command List 1

C   starts COPY command

B   selects Block option

Press F2 (drop anchor) function key.

Press:

End key   moves cursor to end of text, and
         highlights entire block

Press:

F10 function key   selects the Block and stores
         it in the program's copy buffer

The next operation is to unload the standard paragraph and load in the book list again. Press:

4   displays Command list 4

U   starts UNLOAD command
         and clears screen

Press:

L   starts LOAD command

The arrow indicator is pointing to booklist, so press:

RETURN   loads booklist onto screen

Press the PgDn key which moves the cursor down one screen.

Press the End key which moves cursor two lines below
document.

INSERTING THE STANDARD PARAGRAPH INTO THE BOOK LIST

Now you will insert the standard paragraph which is in the
program copy buffer. Press:

1   displays Command list 1

I   starts INSERT command

The standard paragraph has now been inserted into the book
list document.

REPLACING TEXT

It has come to your attention that the name of the group is
incorrect. The title of the organization should read **GROUP**
and not **CLUB**.

To replace all instances of **CLUB** with **GROUP**, press:

R   starts REPLACE command

Press the Caps Lock key once and type:

CLUB   text to be replaced

RETURN   requests replacement text

Type:

GROUP   replacement text

RETURN   displays options

G	selects Global option
RETURN	replaces all occurrences of CLUB with the word GROUP

Your screen should now look like Figure 3.

SAVING THE COMBINED DOCUMENT

Now you must save the booklist, which now includes the
standard paragraph. Press:

4	displays Command list 4
S	starts SAVE command
booklist	filename
RETURN	displays message: File of that name exists. Overwrite (y/n)
Yes	Yes

The file containing the standard paragraph needs to be
corrected, so that the next time you use it, it will contain the
replacement word **GROUP**.

To unload the booklist, press:

U	starts UNLOAD command and clears screen

To load the standard paragraph, press:

L	starts LOAD command
stdpara	filename
RETURN	loads the stdpara onto your screen

SCHEDULE OF READINGS FOR THE GREAT BOOKS DISCUSSION GROUP

Text:	Author:
<u>January readings:</u>	
The Loneliness of the Long Distance Runner	Sillitoe
The Visit to the Museum	Nabakov
<u>February readings:</u>	
The Tempest (Act One)	Shakespeare
Heart of Darkness	Conrad
<u>March readings:</u>	
Death in Venice	Mann
The World as Will and Idea	Schopenhauer

Book lovers of all ages are welcome at the GREAT BOOKS DISCUSSION GROUP meetings. All that is required is that you read the selection to be discussed. Meetings are held at the home of Mr. and Mrs. Henri Phillips, 101 Kerchel Street, Lakewood, Ohio, at 7:30 p.m., on the first and third Wednesdays of every month. For further information on the reading selections, call Mae or Henri Phillips at 555-1134.

Figure 3

Press:

1	displays Command list 1
R	starts REPLACE command

Observe that Smart Word Processor has remembered the text
to be replaced, and **Enter search text ["CLUB"]** is displayed.
Just press:

RETURN	displays: Enter replacement text ["GROUP"]

Again just press:

RETURN	displays: Enter replace options ["G"]

Again just press:

RETURN	replaces all occurrences of **CLUB** with the word **GROUP**

You need to save the corrected standard paragraph. Press:

4	displays Command list 4
S	starts SAVE command
stdpara	filename
RETURN	displays message: File of that name exists. Overwrite (y/n)
Yes	Yes

PRINTING

To print the book notice, be sure your printer is turned on
and then press:

1	displays Command List 1

P	starts PRINT command
E	selects Enhanced option
booklist	name of file to print
RETURN	displays: Enter number of copies

If you wish only one copy, press RETURN.

If you wish, for example, 10 copies for distribution, type the number 10, and then press RETURN.

In this case, you can bypass the prompt: Enter start page number:, so just press:

RETURN	prints document

EXERCISE 4
INSERTING A GRAPH INTO A
WORD PROCESSING DOCUMENT

DESCRIPTION

Smart System allows the insertion of a graph into a word
processing document.

In this exercise, you will create a spreadsheet containing
statistics. You will then define and generate two graphs, a
Bar/Line and a 3-D Pie graph, which will reference
particular portions of the spreadsheet statistics.

A word processing document will be created, into which the
3-D Pie graph will be inserted. Finally, the document will be
printed out, which will include space for the 3-D Pie graph.

This exercise was created on a computer without a color
graphics board.

OPERATIONS PERFORMED

Setting Up The Spreadsheet

Entering Values Into The Spreadsheet

Creating (Defining) A Bar/Line Graph

Generating The Bar/Line Graph

Viewing A Graph

Printing The Bar/Line Graph

Creating (Defining) A 3-D Pie Graph

Generating The 3-D Pie Graph

Viewing The 3-D Pie Graph

Printing The 3-D Pie Graph

Creating A Word Processing Document

Inserting The 3-D Pie Graph Into The Word Processing Document

Saving The Document Containing The Graph

Printing The Document Including Space For The Graph

COMMANDS

GRAPHICS
JUSTIFY
MARKER
PRINT
REFORMAT
SAVE

SETTING UP THE SPREADSHEET

When Smart Spreadsheet is first loaded into your computer, the prompt **Enter:** is displayed at the bottom of your screen. This means you can begin entering data.

Using the following directions, set up your worksheet by copying Figure 1 below exactly as it is illustrated, retaining exact row and column locations of all information.

		1	2	3	4	5
1		PhDs Earned by Tested Groups				
2						
3		American	European	Mexican	Asian	
4	1950	35	20	0	3	
5	1960	575	125	35	.13	
6	1970	2250	700	50	3000	
7	1980	5500	1000	230	11000	

Figure 1

After typing in a label, you may enter the label by moving
the cursor to the next typing location, and the label will be
entered and left-justified.

Place your cursor on R1C2 and type the labels in Rows 1 and
3.

The labels in Row 3 need to be centered, using the JUSTIFY
command.

NOTE

Before starting any command, you must have
displayed on the bottom of your screen a Command
List. If it is not, press the Escape key which will
bring up the Command List. Then press 1,2,3,4 or 5,
depending on which list you want.

Place your cursor on R3C2 and press:

Esc 3   displays Command List 3

J   starts JUSTIFY command

C   selects Center option

R   selects Row option

RETURN   enters the row the cursor
               is on as the row to be formatted

Next place your cursor on R4C1 and press:

Esc   returns to Enter mode

"   double quotation mark, prepares
                       cell for text information

1950   text to entered

RETURN   enters the text

NOTE

When entering text which begins with a number
(1950), it is necessary to type a double quotation mark
(") first. This tells the computer that the number is to
be considered as text, instead of as a value.

Move your cursor to R5C1 and continue entering the labels
in Column 1, remembering to type a double quotation mark
(") before each entry.

ENTERING VALUES INTO THE SPREADSHEET

Next you will enter the *values* in Columns 2, 3, 4 and 5.
Later, you will format those values so they will be displayed
without decimal places and commas.

Place your cursor on R4C2 and begin entering the values in
Columns 2 through 5.

To format the values so they will be displayed without
decimal places and commas,

Place your cursor on R4C2 and press:

Esc   displays Command List 3

R   starts REFORMAT command

C   select Columns option

4   number of columns to be formatted

RETURN   displays options

N   selects Numeric option

N   selects Normal option

N	selects Nocommas option
0	zero, number of decimal places
RETURN	executes the command

Your spreadsheet should look like Figure 1.

Now you will need to save your worksheet. Press:

4	displays Command List 4
S	starts SAVE command
PHDS	filename
RETURN	saves the worksheet

CREATING (DEFINING) A BAR/LINE GRAPH

Now you will create a simple Bar/Line graph of the 1950 statistics in the spreadsheet. This graph is illustrated in Figure 2. Press:

2	displays Command List 2
G	starts GRAPHICS command
D	selects Define option
Type:	
Asians	graphics definition name
RETURN	displays General Graph Definition screen

PhDs Earned by Tested Groups
American
European
Mexican
Asian
0
6
12
18
24
30
36
PhDs Earned — 1950s

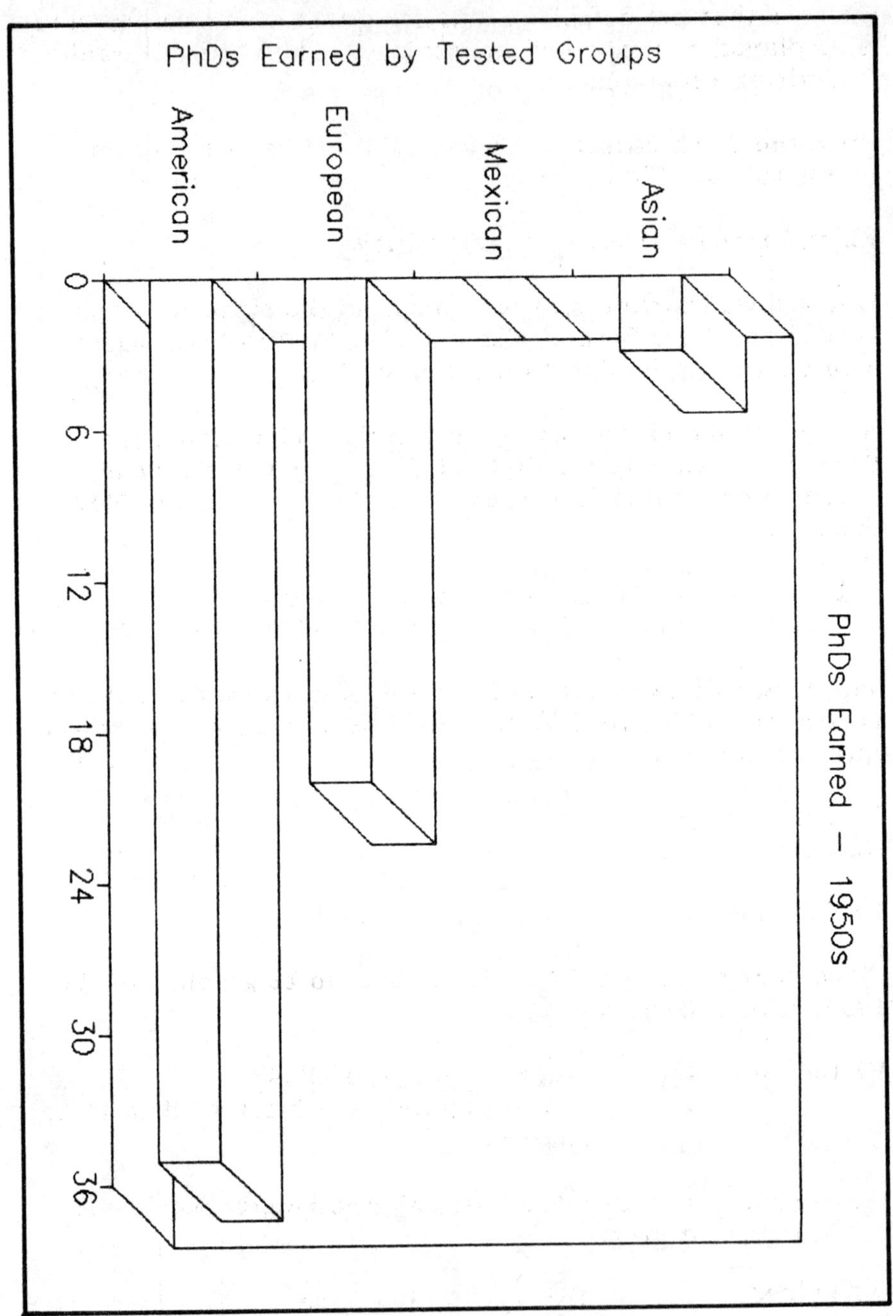

Figure 2

Observe that the definition name (asians) which you entered is displayed at the top of the screen, to the right of Graph Definition File name.

Press the down cursor key once. The indicator arrow now points to Main Title. Type:

PhDs Earned - 1950s   main title

In the lower portion of your screen, to the right of Graph border and Page Border, Yes is highlighted in both places. You do want a border, so leave it as it is.

At the bottom of the screen, to the right of Graph Type:, Bar/Line is already highlighted. Since this is the type of graph to be created in this exercise, do not change it. Now press:

PgDn   PgDn key, displays next screen,
              the Bar-Line Graph Definition screen

You now will enter the range of the data block you wish to be graphed. (This information *must* be entered whenever you create a graph of any type.)

In this exercise, we will graph the information on Row 4, the statistics pertaining to the 1950s. Press:

F6 function key   displays spreadsheet

Place your cursor on R4C2, first value to be graphed in the 1950s row, and press:

F2 function key   drops anchor, and allows
                         you to highlight the block of data to be
                         graphed

Move your cursor to R4C5, last value to be graphed in the 1950s row, and press:

RETURN   displays the Bar-Line
                Graph Definition screen again

Observe that the data block you just defined is now displayed as r4c2:5 directly underneath the words Data Block, at the top of the screen.

Next the X-axis title block needs to be defined.

Press your down cursor key 6 times so that the indicator arrow is pointing to X-Axis title block:

Press:

F6 function key   displays spreadsheet

Place your cursor on R3C2, American, first label in X-axis title block. Press:

F2 function key   (drops anchor)

Move your cursor to R3C5, Asian, last label in X-axis title block. Press:

RETURN   enters X-Axis title block and
                          displays Bar-Line Graph Definition
                          screen again

The cursor has automatically moved down to the next line, the X-Axis title. To enter a title for the X-axis, type:

PhDs Earned by Tested Groups   X-Axis Title

Now press the down cursor key twice so that the indicator arrow is pointing to Options: No Yes

To select Yes, press the SpaceBar once to highlight it. Then press:

RETURN   displays Bar-Line Graph Options
                          screen, with arrow indicator pointing to
                          Bar dimension:

To select the 3-dimensional option, press the SpaceBar once. The highlight is now on 3-dimensional.

Press the down arrow cursor key once so that the indicator
arrow is pointing to Bar orientation.

To select the Horizontal option, press the SpaceBar once. The
highlight is now on Horizontal.

Press the down arrow cursor key twice so that the indicator
arrow is pointing to Legend position.

To select the Bottom option, press the SpaceBar once. The
highlight is now on Bottom.

You have now defined a simple Bar-Line graph, so press:

F10 function key   displays the spreadsheet on
                                your screen, and Command List 2

GENERATING THE BAR/LINE GRAPH

The next operation is to Generate the graph so that it can be
displayed on the screen. It also must be Generated so that
later, in this exercise, it can be incorporated into a word
processing document. Press:

G   starts GRAPHICS command

G   selects Generate option

Asians   graphics definition filename

RETURN   displays Select option:
                Black/white   Color

NOTE

If you are using a monochrome graphics monitor,
press:

B   selects Black/white option

If you are using a color graphics
monitor, press:

C   selects Color option

For this exercise, B was selected.

After you have pressed either B or C, the screen will display:
To save screen, enter screen name:

You can ignore this prompt, so press:

RETURN   displays the prompt:
                           Place Graphics diskette in drive, enter
                           any key
                           Note: This message is displayed only if
                           you have a floppy disk system.

Remove the Smart Spreadsheet diskette No. 1, and replace it
with the Smart *Spreadsheet Graphics* diskette No. 2, and press:

RETURN   completes Generation process

NOTE

If an error message is returned, the graph cannot be
displayed on the screen. (Refer to the Smart System
manual, Systems Commands, Appendix B, Page B-1).

Press the Escape key to eliminate the message, and
respond to the prompts regarding the changing of
program disks in the disk drive before continuing
with this exercise.

VIEWING A GRAPH

To view the graph on your screen, press:

G   starts GRAPHICS command

V   selects View option

Asians   graph filename

RETURN   displays options

I   selects Instant option
                            and displays graph

NOTE

If you are using a monochrome monitor, the
following, or similar, message will be displayed:
Cannot display graphics on monochrome screen.

Although the graph cannot be viewed in this instance,
you will be able to "view" it by printing it out.

Press:

F10 function key   displays spreadsheet

PRINTING THE BAR/LINE GRAPH

The next operation is to print out the graph. To do this, you
must have a printer which is fully supported by SMART.

From Command List 2, select the GRAPHICS command by
pressing:

G   starts GRAPHICS command

M   selects Matrix-Print option

Asians   graphics filename

RETURN   displays:
                          Place Graphics diskette in drive, enter
                          any key

Remove the Spreadsheet No. 1 disk, and replace it with
Spreadsheet No. 2 (graphics) disk.

Be sure your printer is turned on, and press:

RETURN   prints the graph after a
                          short wait

NOTE

While you are waiting for printing to commence, you
will see displayed at the bottom of the screen the
message:
Drawing to printer buffer, pass 1 of 2.

The printer will soon begin printing.

When it pauses again, you will see displayed at the
bottom of the screen the message:
Drawing to printer buffer, pass 2 of 2.

After a short pause, printing will commence again.

Your printed out graph should look like the one illustrated
in Figure 2.

When printing has ceased, you will see the message: Place
Spreadsheet diskette in drive, enter any key.

Remove the Spreadsheet No. 2 diskette (graphics), replace it
with the Spreadsheet No. 1 diskette, and press:

RETURN   displays Command List 2

CREATING (DEFINING) A 3-D PIE GRAPH

A 3-D Pie graph displays data in the form of a "cake", rather
than a pie. Each piece of data (each cell containing data)
becomes a "slice" of the pie, or rather, a slice of the "cake".
This 3-D Pie graph is illustrated in Figure 3.

We will now create a 3-D Pie graph for the data in the
spreadsheet which refers to the 1980s row, and use some of
the enhancements available in the options. Press:

G   starts GRAPHIC command

D   selects Define option

For this exercise we will call our second graph **pie**. Type:

pie   graphics definition name

RETURN   displays General Graph
                Definition screen

Observe that the definition name (pie) which you just
entered is displayed at the top of the screen.

Press the down cursor key once. The indicator arrow now
points to Main Title. Type:

PhDs Earned - 1980s

Press the right arrow cursor key twice. The cursor is now
located below Size. Type:

L   indicates Large type

NOTE

Previously, when you were defining the Bar Graph,
you left this option blank. so the program used the
default size, which is medium.

PhDs Earned – 1980s
Survey by Pandings Institute
Asian
American
European
Mexican
62.0%
31.0%
5.6%
1.3%

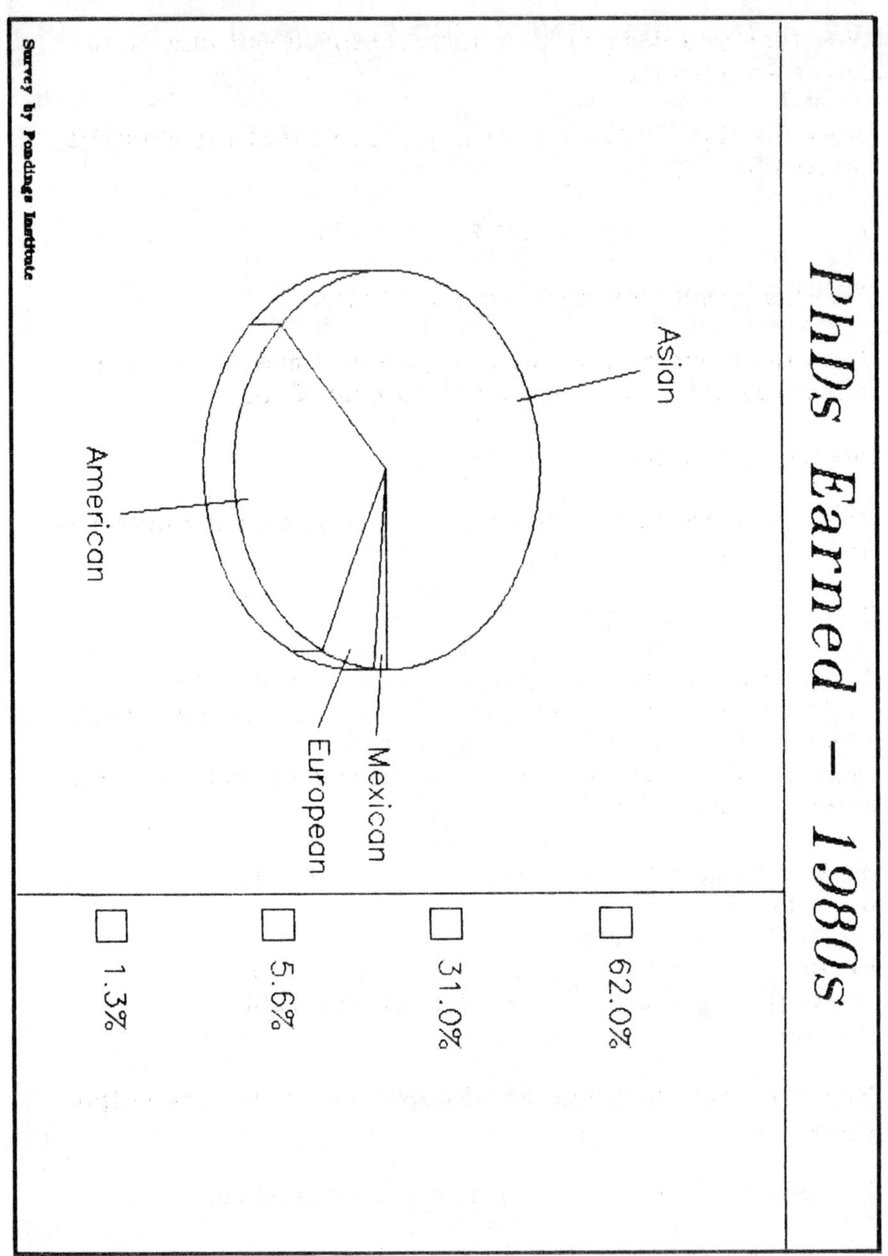

Figure 3

This time you wish to have the title displayed in a more dramatic typeface.

Press the right arrow cursor key once so that the cursor is below Font. Type:

5   selects Italics Roman bold

For this graph, you will add a Footnote.

Press the down arrow cursor key three times so that the arrow indicator is pointing to Footnote. Type:

Survey by Pondings Institute

Press the right arrow cursor key twice so that the cursor is underneath Font. Type:

2   selects Roman typeface

To the right of Graph border and Page Border, Yes is highlighted. You do want a border, so don't change anything.

Press the down arrow cursor key 5 times so that the indicator arrow is pointing to Graph type:

To select the Pie option, press the Spacebar once which will highlight Pie. Then press:

PgDn   PgDn key, displays next screen,
                     the Pie Chart Definition screen

You need now to define the Legend/Labels for the graph. Press:

F6 function key   displays spreadsheet

Place your cursor on R3C2, first label, American. Press:

F2 function key   drops anchor, and allows you
                                     to define the rest of the labels

Move your cursor to R3C5, Asian, last label, and press:

RETURN   enters Legend/Label
                      information and displays Pie Chart
                      Definition screen again

You now must enter the range of the data block you wish to
be graphed. (This information *must* be entered.)

In this exercise, we will graph the information on Row 7, the
statistics pertaining to the 1980s.

Press the down arrow cursor key until the arrow indicator is
pointing to Data block, and then press:

F6 function key   displays spreadsheet

Place your cursor on R7C2, first value in 1980s row, and
press:

F2 function key   drops anchor, and allows
                      you to highlight the block of
                      data to be graphed

Move your cursor to R7C5, last value 1980s row, and press:

RETURN   displays the Pie Chart
                      Definition screen again

Observe that the data block you defined is displayed as
r7c2:5 directly to the right of the words Data Block, at the
bottom of the screen.

The arrow indicator is now pointing to Options: No Yes.

Press the Spacebar once to highlight the Yes. Then press:

PgDn   displays Pie Chart Options

You can now make the "pie" look more like a "cake", so press:

Spacebar   moves highlight to
                          3-dimensional

In order to have the labels you defined earlier displayed in
the 3-D Pie graph, you must reference them. To do this,

Press the down arrow cursor key once so that the arrow
indicator points to Slice labels, and press:

Spacebar Spacebar   highlights Text

Press the down arrow cursor key once so that the arrow
indicator points to Legend type, and press:

Spacebar   highlights Percentages

Press the down arrow cursor key once so that the arrow
indicator points to Sort slices, and press:

Spacebar Spacebar   highlights Descending

Selecting Descending sort order will cause the pie to be
displayed with the largest values first, and then the next
largest, etc., ending with the smallest value. In this survey,
Descending order might be an interesting way to present the
statistics.

The last option will be ignored in this exercise, so just press:

F10 function key   displays spreadsheet

GENERATING THE 3-D PIE GRAPH

The next operation is to Generate the 3-D Pie graph so that
it can be displayed on the screen. It also must be Generated
so that later, if you choose, you can incorporate it into a
word processing document. Press:

G   starts GRAPHIC command

G   selects Generate option

pie   graphics definition filename

RETURN   displays Select option:
                        Black/white   Color

NOTE

If you are using a monochrome graphics monitor,
press:

B   selects Black/white option

If you are using a color graphics
monitor, press:

C   selects Color option

After you have pressed either B or C, the screen will display:

To save screen, enter screen name:

You can ignore this prompt, so press:

RETURN   displays the prompt:
                        Place Graphics diskette in drive, enter
                        any key

                        Note: This message is displayed if you
                        have a floppy disk system

Remove the Smart Spreadsheet diskette No. 1.

Replace it with the Smart *Spreadsheet Graphics* diskette No.
2.

Press:

RETURN   completes Generation process

NOTE

If an error message is returned, the graph cannot be displayed on the screen.

Refer to the Smart System manual, Systems Command, Appendix B, Page B-1.

VIEWING THE 3-D PIE GRAPH

To view the graph on your screen, press:

G	starts GRAPHICS command
V	selects View option
pie	graph filename
RETURN	displays options
I	selects Instant option

NOTE

If an error message is returned, the graph cannot be displayed on the screen. (Refer to the Smart System manual, Systems Commands, Appendix B, Page B-1).

Press the Escape key to eliminate the message, and respond to the prompts regarding the changing of program disks in the disk drive before continuing with this exercise.

Press:

F10 function key	displays spreadsheet

PRINTING THE 3-D PIE GRAPH

The next operation is to print out the 3-D Pie graph.

From Command List 2, select GRAPHICS by pressing:

G   starts GRAPHICS command

M   selects Matrix-Print option

pie   graphics filename

RETURN   displays:
                     Place Graphics diskette in drive, enter
                     any key

Remove the Spreadsheet No. 1 disk, and replace it with
Spreadsheet No. 2 (graphics) disk.

Be sure your printer is turned on, and press:

RETURN   prints the 3-D Pie graph after
                     a short wait

NOTE

While you are waiting for printing to commence, you
will see displayed at the bottom of the screen the
message:
Drawing to printer buffer, pass 1 of 2.

The printer will soon begin printing.

When it pauses again, you will see displayed at the
bottom of the screen the message:
Drawing to printer buffer, pass 2 of 2.

After a short pause, printing will commence again.

Your 3-D Pie graph should look like the one illustrated in
Figure 3.

The message: **Place Spreadsheet Diskette in drive, enter any
key**, is displayed.

Remove the Spreadsheet diskette No. 2 (graphics).

Replace it with the Spreadsheet diskette No. 1, and press:

RETURN   displays spreadsheet

CREATING A WORD PROCESSING DOCUMENT

The next operation is to create a word processing document
explaining the 3-D Pie graph.

Then you will incorporate the 3-D Pie graph into the text of
the word processing document.

To access the Smart Word Processor, press:

F10 function key   displays program options

W   selects Wordprocessor option

Remove Smart Spreadsheet No. 1 disk from the disk drive.

Replace it with Smart Word Processor disk.

RETURN   loads Word Processor program
                          and displays a blank screen

NOTE

If you see the message: Macro file not found, just
press RETURN to eliminate the message.

Using the following instructions, type in the document which
is illustrated in Figure 4.

Press the Tab key three times to indent the heading you are
about to type. Then press:

CAPS LOCK   turns on Caps Lock toggle

Type:

PONDINGS INSTITUTE SURVEY

Turn off the CAPS LOCK by pressing it once.

Press RETURN twice to move the cursor down two lines.

Now type in the document illustrated in Figure 4, pressing
RETURN only at the end of each paragraph and at the end
of the document.

The next step is to save the document. Press:

Esc 4   displays Command List 4

S   selects SAVE command

Pondings   filename

RETURN   saves the document

PONDINGS INSTITUTE SURVEY

The findings of the Pondings Institute survey indicate the dramatic rise in the number of PhD degrees in Computer Science attained by the Asian population in the United States, particularly after the end of the Viet Nam War.

The survey finds that in the 1950s three Asian students obtained doctorates in Computer Science. The incidence of doctorate attainment rose slightly in the 1960s, but in the 1970s and 1980s the rise was phenomenal. The statistics pertaining to the 1980s are displayed in the graph contained herein.

The reason for the rapid advance in doctorate achievement is not yet clear. However, further studies are being made to determine why the Asian population, the majority of which immigrated to the United States with slight knowledge of the English language, have been able to surpass other groups in this area of scholastic attainment, considering the fact that they have a particular problem because of their many dialects and the relatively few English instructors versed in multi-dialects.

The Mexican population, because of the bi-lingual classes available, gain knowledge of English soon after arrival in the United States; the European population has a somewhat better advantage, having been exposed to English abroad.

The results of the study should prove extremely interesting. However, at this time, it is not known what time period is being considered for the completion of the study.

Figure 4

INSERTING THE 3-D PIE GRAPH INTO THE WORD PROCESSING DOCUMENT

You have decided to use the second graph you previously created, the 3-D Pie graph, for insertion into the word processing document.

The first thing you must do is to set a Marker in the word processing document, indicating where the graph is to be inserted. To do this,

Place the cursor at the beginning of the third paragraph, on Line 15, and press:

3	displays Command List 3
M	starts MARKER command
S	selects Set option
graph	marker name
RETURN	accepts marker name

No marker is visible on your screen; however, it has been stored with the document.

To insert the graph, press:

F4 function key	the Goto key
graph	marker name
RETURN	displays Command List 1
4	displays Command List 4
G	starts GRAPHICS command
I	selects Insert option
pie	graph filename
RETURN	displays options

M   selects Medium option

R   selects Right-Justified option

A shaded area is now displayed within the document.

In the center of the shaded area, **b:pie.scn** is displayed.

Observe that the text has adjusted itself around the shaded
graph area.

SAVING THE DOCUMENT CONTAINING THE GRAPH

Assuming Command List 4 is still displayed on your screen,
press:

S   starts SAVE command

RETURN   saves the document

PRINTING THE DOCUMENT INCLUDING SPACE FOR THE GRAPH

You are ready to print out your document, which will now
contain space for the 3-D Pie graph.

NOTE

The following directions are for users who DO NOT
have a color graphics board.

Press:

1	displays Command List 1
P	starts PRINT command
N	selects Normal option
pondings	name of file to be printed
RETURN	displays options
P	selects Printer option and displays Enter number of copies:

To print just one copy for this exercise, press:

RETURN	displays: Enter start page number
RETURN	begins printing

NOTE

There will be a printout of the document, including the 3-D Pie graph, if the user has a printer supported by SMART *and* a graphics card.

Your printout will look like Figure 6 on the following page.

PONDINGS INSTITUTE SURVEY

The findings of the Pondings Institute survey indicate the dramatic rise in the number of PhD degrees in Computer Science attained by the Asian population in the United States, particularly after the end of the View Nam War.

The survey finds that in the 1950s three Asian students obtained doctorates in Computer Science. The incidence of doctorate attainment rose slightly in the 1960s, but in the 1970s and 1980s the rise was phenomenal. The statistics pertaining to the 1980s are displayed in the graph contained herein.

The reason for the rapid advance in doctorate achievement is not yet clear. However, further studies are being made to determine why the Asian population, the majority of which immigrated to the United States with slight knowledge of the English language, have been able to

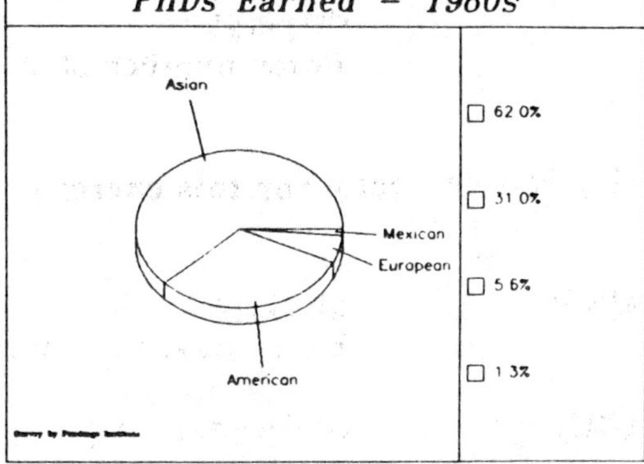

surpass other groups in this area of scholastic attainment, considering the fact that they have a particular problem becuse of their many dialects and the relatively few English instructors versed in multi-dialects.

The Mexican population, because of the bi-lingual classes available, gain knowledge of English soon after arrival in the United States; the European population has a somewhat better advantage, having been exposed to English abroad.

The results of the study should prove extremely interesting. However, at this time, it is not known what time period is being considered for the completion of the study.

Figure 6

EXERCISE 5
MERGING A WORD PROCESSING DOCUMENT
WITH A DATABASE

DESCRIPTION

In this exercise a basic form letter will be created using the
Smart Word Processor. Next a database, consisting of names
and addresses, will be created, using the Smart Data
Manager.

The database will be merged with the form letter, and a
letter will be printed out for each of the names in the
database. Each letter will contain a different name and
address as well as information pertinent to that particular
letter.

OPERATIONS PERFORMED

Creating A Form Letter And Inserting Variables

Saving The Letter

Creating A Database

Entering Data Into The Database

Browsing The Database

Saving The Database

Sending The Database To The Word Processor

Merging The Database and The Letter

COMMANDS

BROWSE
CREATE
ENTER
LOAD
MERGE
PRINT
SAVE
SEND
VISIBLE

CREATING A FORM LETTER AND INSERTING VARIABLES

After the Smart Word Processor program has been loaded into your computer, a diamond symbol is displayed at the upper left of the screen, indicating end of document.

To make the diamond symbol (and future paragraph marks) invisible, press:

Esc   displays Command list 1

2   displays Command list 2

V   starts VISIBLE command

P   selects Paragraph-Marks option
                        and makes the diamond symbol
                        invisible, as well as future paragraph
                        marks

Press:

Esc   returns to Text-Entry mode

You are now ready to *use the following directions* for typing in the document (the business form letter), and to insert the variable names which will later extract the appropriate information from a database. The letter is illustrated in Figure 1.

```
July 1, 1985

<Company>
<Street Address>
<City>
<State>
<Zip>

Attn:  <Name>

Dear <Salutation>

This  letter is to let you know that a representative of  our
firm will be in <City> the second week of August.   If  there
are any questions concerning our products, please schedule an
appointment with our representative during that time  period.
[RETURN] [RETURN]
There  have  been a series of important changes made  in  the
last  six  months concerning marketing and  distribution,  of
which you should be aware.  The changes will benefit both you
and potential customers in <State>.   Please try to  schedule
time to meet with our representative.  [RETURN] [RETURN]

Thank you.  [RETURN] [RETURN] [RETURN]


Connie Viola  [RETURN]
Vice-President  [RETURN]
Marketing Division  [RETURN] [RETURN]
```

Figure 1

Leave your cursor where it is, at the upper left of the screen, and type:

July 1, 1985

RETURN RETURN   moves cursor down to Line 3

You will now insert the first variable name which will later extract the appropriate data from a database which you will be creating later in this exercise.

Hold down the Control key and press:

J   inserts <<

Type:

Company   first database field

Hold down the Control key and press:

K   inserts >>

NOTE

The << and >> symbols *must* be used to enclose the variable field name.

Later, Smart Word Processor will be reading these << and >> symbols to extract the proper information from the database, and will print it into this Word Processor letter.

Press:

RETURN   moves cursor to Line 4

Hold down the Control key and press:

J   inserts <<

Type:

Street Address   second field

Hold down the Control key and press:

K   inserts >>

RETURN   moves cursor to Line 5

Hold down the Control key and press:

J   inserts <<

Type:

City   third field

Hold down the Control key and press:

K   inserts >>

RETURN   moves cursor to Line 6

Hold down the Control key and press:

J   inserts <<

Type:

State   fourth field

Hold down the Control key and press:

K   inserts >>

RETURN   moves cursor to Line 7

Hold down the Control key and press:

J   inserts <<

Type:

Zip   fifth field

Hold down the Control key and press:

K   inserts >>

RETURN RETURN moves cursor to Line 9.

Type:

Attn:

Press the Spacebar twice to insert two blank spaces. Then
hold down the Control key and press:

J   inserts <<

Type:

Name   sixth field

Hold down the Control key and press:

K   inserts >>

RETURN RETURN moves cursor to Line 11

Type:

Dear

Press the Spacebar once to insert a space. Then hold down
the Control key and press:

J   inserts <<

Type:

Salutation   seventh field

Hold down the Control key and press:

K   inserts >>

Type:

,   (comma)

RETURN RETURN moves the cursor down to Line 13

Type in the letter which is illustrated in Figure 1. When you see RETURN, just press RETURN as many times as indicated.

NOTE

> Our printout (Figure 1) displays the << as <, and the >> as >.
>
> Disregard this printer discrepancy.
>
> When you see < in the Figure, just hold down the Control key and press J.
>
> When you see > in the Figure, hold down the Control key and press K.

When you have completed typing the letter, your screen should look like Figure 1, with the exception, of course, of the << and >> because of the printer discrepancy. See NOTE above.

SAVING THE LETTER

The document must be saved. Press:

Esc   displays Command List 1

4   displays Command List 4

S   starts SAVE command

letter   filename

RETURN   saves the document

CREATING A DATABASE

The next operation is to create a database containing names
and addresses of people to whom the form letter will be sent.
The first step is to access the Smart Data-Manager program.
Press:

F10 function key   displays program options

D   selects Data-Manager option

The message: **Place Data-Manager diskette in drive, enter any
key,** is displayed.

Remove the Smart Word Processor diskette, replace it with
the Smart Data Manager diskette, and press:

RETURN   loads Data-Manager program and
                            displays Command List 1

Press:

C   starts CREATE command

F   selects File option

dealers   filename

RETURN   displays options

V   selects Variable-Length option

N   selects No-Password option

N   selects New option and displays the
                            File Definition screen

Leave the cursor where it is, on the Title field, and type:

Company   name of first field

RETURN   moves cursor to Type column

Type:

A   Alpha, type of entry

The cursor has automatically moved to the Length column.
Type:

15

RETURN   moves cursor back to Title column

Type:

Street Address

RETURN   moves cursor to Type column

Type:

A   Alpha, type of entry

The cursor has automatically moved to the Length column.
Type:

15

RETURN   moves cursor back to Title column

Type:

City

RETURN   moves cursor to Type column

Type:

A   Alpha, type of entry

The cursor has automatically moved to the Length column.
Type:

12

RETURN   moves cursor to Title column

Type:

 State

RETURN   moves cursor to Type column

Type:

A   Alpha, type of entry

The cursor has automatically moved to the Length column.
Type:

2

RETURN   moves cursor to Title column

Type:

 Zip

RETURN   moves cursor to Type column

Type:

A   Alpha, type of entry

The cursor has automatically moved to the Length column.
Type:

5

RETURN   moves cursor to Title column

Type:

 Name

RETURN   moves cursor to Type column

Type:

A   Alpha, type of entry

The cursor automatically moves to Length column. Type:

14

RETURN   moves cursor back to Title column

Type:

 Salutation

RETURN   moves cursor to Type column

Type:

A   Alpha, type of entry

The cursor automatically moves to Length column. Type:

12

RETURN   moves cursor back to Title column

You are finished defining the file so press:

F10 function key
       displays message: Are you finished
       defining file (y/n)

Type:

Y   Yes

The program now saves the file definition and displays
another message:

Do you want to define a key field (y/n)

Type:

N   No

The screen now displays the fields in column format, and
Command List 1 is displayed.

Your screen should look like Figure 2 below.

Company
Street Address
City
State
Zip
Name
Salutation

Figure 2

ENTERING DATA INTO THE DATABASE

To enter data into the database, press:

E   starts ENTER command and displays
                        Record 1

Leave the cursor where it is and type:

TimFab Co

RETURN   moves cursor to next line

Continue entering the data which is illustrated below,
pressing RETURN only where indicated.

5500 El Camino [RETURN]
Portland [RETURN]
CA   (Record 1)
94022
Joe Moore [RETURN]
Mr. Moore [RETURN]

Alder Co [RETURN]
12 Nathan St [RETURN]
Julietown [RETURN]
OR   (Record 2)
94311
Hazel Woodward
Ms. Woodward

Susaner Co [RETURN]
P O Box 170 [RETURN]
Spokane [RETURN]
WA   (Record 3)
84302
Joan Bowyer [RETURN]
Ms. Bowyer [RETURN]

Musica Co [RETURN]
4 Pianola Rd [RETURN]
Hindemith [RETURN]
MA   (Record 4)
20233
Bruce Edward [RETURN]
Mr. Edward [RETURN]

LeeAnn Inc [RETURN]
10 Zoo Hwy [RETURN]
Carpenter [RETURN]
NH   (Record 5)
03278
Jessie Daniel [RETURN]
Mr. Daniel [RETURN]

After the records have been typed in, and the last RETURN pressed, a blank Record 6 is displayed. Press:

F10 function key   displays Command List 1

BROWSING THE DATABASE

To see all the records in BROWSE mode, press:

B   starts BROWSE command

A   selects All option and displays
                        all records

SAVING THE DATABASE

To save the database, press:

4   displays Command List 4

S   starts SAVE command and saves
                        database

SENDING THE DATABASE TO THE WORD PROCESSOR

The next operation is to send the database to the word processor, using the SEND command. Press:

5   displays Command List 5

S   starts SEND command

A   selects All option and displays
                        program options

W   selects Wordprocessor option and
                        displays Available fields

In the Available fields box at the bottom of the screen, the arrow indicator is pointing to the first field, Company. Press:

F6 function key   selects the first field and
                                   displays [1;

Press the right arrow cursor key once so that the arrow indicator is pointing to the second field, Street Address, and press:

F6 function key   selects the second field and
                                   displays [1;2;

Press the right arrow cursor key once so that the arrow indicator is pointing to the third field, City, and press:

F6 function key   selects the third field and
                                   displays [1;2;3;

Press the left arrow cursor key twice; then press the down arrow cursor key once, so that the arrow indicator is pointing to the fourth field, State, and press:

F6 function key   selects the fourth field and
                                   displays [1;2;3;4;

Press the right arrow cursor key once so that the arrow indicator is pointing to the fifth field, Zip, and press:

F6 function key   selects fifth field and
                                   displays [1;2;3;4;5;

Press the right arrow cursor key once so that the arrow indicator is pointing to the sixth field, Name, and press:

F6 function key   selects sixth field and
                                   displays [1;2;3;4;5;6;

Press the left arrow cursor key twice. Then press the down arrow cursor key once, so that the arrow indicator is pointing to the seventh field, Salutation, and press:

F6 function key   selects seventh field and
                        displays [1;2;3;4;5;6;7;

RETURN   ends selection of fields and
                        displays options

D   selects Data option and displays:
                        Enter project file for next application

You can bypass this prompt, so just press:

RETURN   unloads database and displays:
                        **Place Wordprocessor diskette in drive,
                        enter any key**

Remove the Smart Data Manager diskette, replace it with the Smart Word Processor diskette, and press:

RETURN   sends data to word processor

After the data has been sent to the word processor, the word processing screen is displayed.

The database data has now been sent to the Smart Word Processor and is stored in a disk file under the name of the data file (dealers) with the extension IFF.

MERGING THE DATABASE AND THE LETTER

The next operation is to merge the database names and addresses into the form letter so that they will print out.

First the letter must be loaded onto the screen. Press:

Esc 4   displays Command List 4

L   starts LOAD command

Type:

letter   file to be loaded

RETURN   loads letter onto the screen

The last operation is to merge the database with the letter.
Be sure your printer is turned on, and then press:

M   starts MERGE command

F   selects File option

N   selects Normal option and displays:
                  Enter filename:

RETURN   merges the two files and
                  prints the five letters

The first letter should look like Figure 3.

```
July 1, 1985

TimFab Co
5500 El Camino
Portland
CA
94022

Attn:  Joe Moore

Dear Mr. Moore,

This  letter is to let you know that a representative of  our
firm will be in Portland the second week of August.  If there
are any questions concerning our products, please schedule an
appointment with our representative during that time period.

There  have  been a series of important changes made  in  the
last  six  months concerning marketing and  distribution,  of
which you should be aware.  The changes will benefit both you
and potential customers in CA. Please try to schedule time to
meet with our representative.

Thank you.


Connie Viola
Vice-President
Marketing Division
```

Figure 3

EXERCISE 6
COST RECOVERY SPREADSHEET

DESCRIPTION

This exercise is a cost recovery worksheet, which is set up to determine the investment balance still owing on a purchased item.

Smart Spreadsheet's VCOPY command is used to update the worksheet once a month with rental income received, which reduces the original purchase balance. Each time the worksheet is updated, the number of months the items have been in service is also calculated.

After the balance has been recovered, the profit being made on the item, and the total number of months the item has been in service, is then reported.

OPERATIONS PERFORMED

Setting up the Worksheet Format

Naming Cells

Entering Mathematical Formulas

Making Worksheet Entries

Updating the Worksheet

Saving

Printing

COMMANDS

AUTO-RECALC
BLANK
COPY
JUSTIFY
NAME
PRINT
REFORMAT
SAVE
VCOPY
WIDTH

FUNCTIONS

ABS
MAX
MIN
SUM

SETTING UP WORKSHEET FORMAT

Using the following directions, set up your worksheet by copying Figure 1 exactly as it is illustrated, retaining exact row and column locations of all information.

NOTE

Before starting any command, you must have displayed on the bottom of your screen a Command List. If it is not, press the Escape key which will bring up the Command List. Then press 1, 2, 3, 4 or 5, depending on which list you want.

The SMART SPREADSHEET worksheet format contains columns which are ten characters wide when it is first entered into the computer.

In this exercise you will need to expand Column 1 so that it will be 14 characters wide, and contract Column 5 so that it will be 7 characters wide, to accommodate their labelling information.

```
          1       2        3       4       5        6        7       8        9
 1
 2      Item   Purchase  Rent   Invest  Mths in  Profit          Work   Area
 3      Name    Price    Rec'd  Balance Service  Margin  Balance Service Margin
   ----------------------------------------------------------------------------
 4
 5
 6
 7
 8
 9
10
11 ============================================================================
12
```

Figure 1

Place your cursor on Column 1 and press:

Esc	displays Command List 1
3	displays Command List 3
W	starts WIDTH command
14	width of column
RETURN	enters width
C	selects Columns option
RETURN	enters the column the cursor is on, to be widened

Move your cursor to Column 5 and press:

W	starts WIDTH command
7	width of column
RETURN	enters width
C	selects Columns option
RETURN	enters the column the cursor is on, to be contracted
Esc	returns to Enter mode

The next operation is to type in your row and column labels. They will be centered later.

After typing in a label, you may enter the label by moving the cursor to the next typing location, and the label will be entered and left-justified.

NOTE

To type in the label **Work Area** in Row 1,

Place your cursor on R1C7 and press the Spacebar 7 times and type:

Work

Press the Spacebar 4 times and type:

Area

After you have entered all the labels, you will center them in their appropriate columns.

Place your cursor on Row 1, Column 1, and display Command List 3 by pressing:

Esc 3	displays Command List 3
J	starts JUSTIFY command
C	selects Center option
B	selects Block option

Move your cursor to Row 2, Column 9, highlighting the area to be centered, and press:

RETURN	centers the labels
Esc	returns to Enter mode

Now let's place a dashed line across Row 3.

Place your cursor on R3C1 and press:

\	Backslash, starts Repeat label and displays a dashed line across Column 1
RETURN	enters the dashed line

Next copy the dashed line just entered in R3C1, using the Copy command in Command List 1. Press:

Esc 1	displays Command List 1
C	starts COPY command
R	selects Right option
S	selects Single-Cell option
8	number of copies
RETURN	copies dashed line across the row to Column 9
Esc	returns to Enter mode

To enter the double-dashed line on Row 11,

Place your cursor on R11C1 and press:

\	Backslash, starts Repeat label and displays a dashed line across Column 1
=	equal sign, label to be repeated
RETURN	enters the double-dashed line

Next copy the double-dashed line just entered in R11C1, using the Copy command in Command List 1. Press:

Esc 1	displays Command List 1
C	starts COPY command
R	selects Right option
S	selects Single-Cell option

8	number of copies
RETURN	copies double-dashed line across the row to Column 9

NAMING CELLS

Now that the labels are typed in, we will name some of the cells to make it easier when using them in formulas and in updating the worksheet.

The first group of cells to be named is the Rent Rec'd column.

Place your cursor on R4C3 and press:

1	displays Command List 1
N	starts NAME command
D	selects Define option
BLRENT	name of cells
RETURN	displays Enter Definition for this name:

Move the cursor to R10C3. Screen will reverse to indicate area being named. Press:

RETURN	executes the command and names the selected cells

The second set of cells to name is the Invest Balance, Mths in Service and Profit Margin columns.

Place your cursor on R4C4 and press:

N	starts NAME command

D	selects Define option
UPDATE	name of cells
RETURN	displays Enter Definition for this name:

Move the cursor to R10C6. Screen will reverse to indicate area being named. Press:

RETURN	executes the command and names the selected cells

Your worksheet should now look like Figure 1.

ENTERING MATHEMATICAL FORMULAS

You will now begin entering mathematical formulas that will establish the relationships between column and row positions. The formulas and their locations are illustrated in Figure 2.

Formula one, at the bottom of Purchase Price column, adds the amount of the purchase prices between the double and single dashed lines.

Place your cursor on R12C2 and press:

Esc	returns to Enter mode
=	displays Enter formula:
SUM(	adds values in the following list

Press the up arrow once to move cursor to double dashed line; r11c2 is displayed.

.	Press the F2 (drop anchor) function key.

Press up arrow 8 times to move cursor to single dashed line. r3:11c2 is displayed. Type:

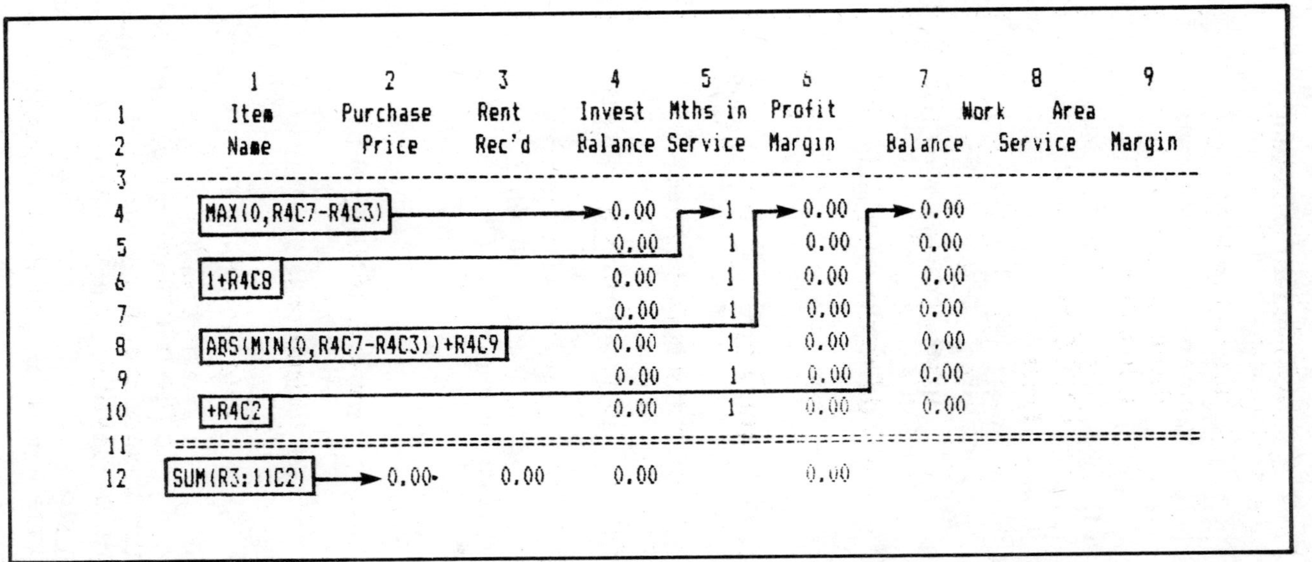

	1	2	3	4	5	6	7	8	9
	Item	Purchase	Rent	Invest	Mths in	Profit		Work	Area
	Name	Price	Rec'd	Balance	Service	Margin	Balance	Service	Margin
3	---								
4	MAX(0,R4C7-R4C3)			0.00	1	0.00	0.00		
5				0.00	1	0.00	0.00		
6	1+R4C8			0.00	1	0.00	0.00		
7				0.00	1	0.00	0.00		
8	ABS(MIN(0,R4C7-R4C3))+R4C9			0.00	1	0.00	0.00		
9				0.00	1	0.00	0.00		
10	+R4C2			0.00	1	0.00	0.00		
11	===								
12	SUM(R3:11C2)	0.00-	0.00	0.00		0.00			

Figure 2

)	right parenthesis, closes the list
RETURN	enters the formula

The next operation is to copy the formula just entered across the row into the Rent Rec'd, Invest Balance and Profit Margin rows.

Leave your cursor on R12C2 and press:

Esc 1	displays Command List 1
C	starts COPY command
R	selects Right option
S	selects Single-Cell option
4	number of copies
RETURN	copies formula across the row into Columns 3, 4, 5 and 6

The formula is not needed in Column 5, the Mths in Service column, so it must be blanked out.

Place your cursor on R12C5 and press:

B	starts BLANK command
B	selects Block option
RETURN	deletes formula from R12C5

Formula two, in the Invest Balance column, provides a means for the Invest Balance column to display the unrecovered purchase cost of each item listed. When the full purchase cost of each piece of equipment is recovered, the Invest Balance column will display $0.00 opposite that item.

Place your cursor on R4C4 and press:

Esc	returns to Enter mode

=   displays Enter formula:

MAX(selects maximum value from
                        the following list

0   zero value

,   comma, separates values
                        in list

Press the right arrow 3 times to move cursor to Work Area:
Balance. r4c7 is displayed. Type:

-                       subtracts

Press left arrow once to move cursor to Rent Rec'd column.
r4c3 is displayed. Type:

)   right parenthesis, closes
                        the list

RETURN   enters the formula

Formula three, in the Mths In Service column, advances the
months in service by one each time the updating operation is
performed.

Place your cursor on R4C5 and type:

=   displays Enter formula:

1   value

+   adds

Press right arrow 3 times to move cursor to Work Area,
Service. r4c8 is displayed.

RETURN   enters the formula

The next operation is to format the cell into which you just
entered the formula so that it will be displayed as an integer.

Leave your cursor on R4C5 and press:

Esc 3	displays Command List 3
R	starts REFORMAT command
B	selects Block option
RETURN	enters the cell the cursor is on as the cell to be formatted
N	selects Numeric option
N	selects Normal option
N	selects Nocommas option
0	number of decimal places
RETURN	formats the cell in integers

Formula four, in the Profit Margin column, displays accumulated gross profits when purchase price of item has been recovered.

Place your cursor on R4C6 and press:

Esc	returns to Enter mode
=	displays Enter formula:
ABS(	displays amount as a positive number
MIN(	selects minimum value from the following list
0	zero value
,	comma, separates values in list

Press right arrow once to move cursor to Work Area, Balance. R4C7 is displayed. Type:

subtracts

Press left arrow 3 times to move cursor to Rent Rec'd
column. R4C3 is displayed. Type:

))   right parentheses, closes
                       expressions

+   adds

Press right arrow 3 times to move cursor to Work Area,
Margin. R4C9 is displayed. Press:

RETURN   enters the formula

Formula five, in the Work Area Balance column, displays the
original purchase price. This is only used when first setting
up the worksheet. The formula will be automatically deleted
when updated with the Investment Balance amount.

Place your cursor on R4C7 and type:

=   displays Enter formula:

Press left arrow 5 times to move cursor to Purchase Price.
R4C2 is displayed. Press:

RETURN   enters the formula

The next operation will be to copy the formulas just entered
down the appropriate columns.

Place your cursor on R4C4 and press:

Esc 1   selects Command List 1

C   starts COPY command

F   selects From option

Move the cursor to R4C7. The screen reverses to indicate the
area being copied.

RETURN   enters area to be copied

Move the cursor to R5C4, first cell to copy to and press:

F2 function key (drop anchor)

Move your cursor to R10C7, last cell to copy to, and press:

RETURN   copies formulas down
                  the columns

Your worksheet should now look like Figure 2.

MAKING WORKSHEET ENTRIES

Press Esc to return to Enter mode, and type in the entries in
the Item Name, Purchase Price and Rent Rec'd columns as
illustrated in Figure 3.

NOTE

Do not type into cells which contain formulas, or the
formulas will be erased.

After the entries are typed in, the worksheet must be
calculated. Press:

Esc 5   displays Command List 5

A   starts AUTO-RECALC command

A   selects Automatic option

Press:

F5 function key

          recalculates worksheet.

          Note: Hereafter your worksheet will
          calculate automatically for you.

You need to format portions of the worksheet so that they
will be displayed as currency.

		1	2	3	4	5	6	7	8	9
									Work	Area
1		Item	Purchase	Rent	Invest	Mths in	Profit			
2		Name	Price	Rec'd	Balance	Service	Margin	Balance	Service	Margin
3		------								
4	Hammer	$25.00	$5.00	$20.00	1	$0.00	$25.00		
5	Shovel	$75.00	$15.00	$60.00	1	$0.00	$75.00		
6	Trailer	$1250.00	$75.00	$1175.00	1	$0.00	$1250.00		
7	Bike	$550.00	$25.00	$525.00	1	$0.00	$550.00		
8	Truck	$5500.00	$150.00	$5350.00	1	$0.00	$5500.00		
9	Motor	$125.00	$8.00	$117.00	1	$0.00	$125.00		
10	Ax	$125.00	$5.00	$120.00	1	$0.00	$125.00		
11		======								
12		$7650.00	$283.00	$7367.00		$0.00			

Figure 3

Place your cursor on R4C2, first cell to format in currency, and press:

3	displays Command List 3
R	starts REFORMAT command
B	selects Block option

Move your cursor to R12C4, last cell to format, and press:

RETURN	displays Select option:
C	selects Currency option
N	selects Normal option
N	selects Nocommas option
2	number of decimal places
RETURN	formats the block in currency

The next area to format as currency is the Work Area, Balance column.

Place your cursor on R4C7, first cell to format in currency, and press:

R	starts REFORMAT command
B	selects Block option

Move your cursor to R10C7, last cell to format, and press:

RETURN	displays Select option:
C	selects Currency option
N	selects Normal option
N	selects Nocommas option

2	number of decimal places
RETURN	formats the block in currency

Your worksheet should now look like Figure 3.

Next save the entire worksheet. Press:

4	displays Command List 4
S	selects SAVE command
CR	name of worksheet (CR stands for Cost Recovery)
RETURN	saves the worksheet

WORKSHEET UPDATING

To perform the updating process, you will use the VCOPY command to copy *the values only* in the Invest Balance, Mths in Service and Profit Margin information, which were earlier named UPDATE. These values will be copied to the Work Area's 3 columns.

The worksheet, after updating, is illustrated in Figure 4 below.

Place your cursor on R4C7, first column in Work Area, and press:

1	displays Command List 1
V	starts VCOPY command
F	selects From option

		1	2	3	4	5	6	7	8	9
1		Item	Purchase	Rent	Invest	Mths in	Profit		Work	Area
2		Name	Price	Rec'd	Balance	Service	Margin	Balance	Service	Margin
3		--								
4	Hammer	$25.00		$20.00	2	$0.00	$20.00	1	$0.00	
5	Shovel	$75.00		$60.00	2	$0.00	$60.00	1	$0.00	
6	Trailer	$1250.00		$1175.00	2	$0.00	$1175.00	1	$0.00	
7	Bike	$550.00		$525.00	2	$0.00	$525.00	1	$0.00	
8	Truck	$5500.00		$5350.00	2	$0.00	$5350.00	1	$0.00	
9	Motor	$125.00		$117.00	2	$0.00	$117.00	1	$0.00	
10	Ax	$125.00		$120.00	2	$0.00	$120.00	1	$0.00	
11	==									
12		$7650.00	$0.00	$7367.00		$0.00				

Figure 4

UPDATE   name of block reference
                    to copy from

RETURN   enters the name

RETURN   copies the block

The next operation will be to blank the Rent Rec'd column,
which we previously named BLRENT.

Leave your cursor on any location and press:

B   selects BLANK command

Block   selects Block option

BLRENT   name of cells to be blanked

RETURN   blanks the cells

Your worksheet is updated and should look like Figure 4.

You can now type in the new Rent Rec'd amounts as
illustrated in Figure 5. (Remember to first press the Escape
key to return to the Enter mode.)

After you have typed in the Rent Rec'd amounts (Figure 5),
repeat the updating procedure again, as described under the
paragraph heading WORKSHEET UPDATING.

SAVING

To save your worksheet, press:

Esc 4   displays Command List 4

S   starts SAVE command and
               displays Enter worksheet name:

		1	2	3	4	5	6	7	8	9
1		Item	Purchase	Rent	Invest	Mths in	Profit		Work	Area
2		Name	Price	Rec'd	Balance	Service	Margin	Balance	Service	Margin
3		--------								
4	Hammer	$25.00	21.00	$0.00	2	$1.00	$20.00	1	$0.00
5	Shovel	$75.00	25.00	$35.00	2	$0.00	$60.00	1	$0.00
6	Trailer	$1250.00	100.00	$1075.00	2	$0.00	$1175.00	1	$0.00
7	Bike	$550.00	600.00	$0.00	2	$75.00	$525.00	1	$0.00
8	Truck	$5500.00	225.00	$5125.00	2	$0.00	$5350.00	1	$0.00
9	Motor	$125.00	135.00	$0.00	2	$18.00	$117.00	1	$0.00
10	Ax	$125.00	12.00	$108.00	2	$0.00	$120.00	1	$0.00
11		=========								
12		$7650.00	$1118.00	$6343.00		$94.00			

Figure 5

CR   name of worksheet
                (stands for Cost Recovery)

RETURN   saves the worksheet

If the worksheet was previously saved under the same name, the message Overwrite existing file (y/n) will be displayed.

In response, type Y to save the worksheet in place of the existing one; or type N to save the worksheet under another name, and then follow the prompts.

PRINTING

To print the entire worksheet, in compressed font,

Place your cursor on R1C1 and press:

Esc 1   displays Command List 1

P   starts PRINT command

T   selects Text option

W   selects Worksheet option

P   selects Printer option

C   selects Compressed (font) option

1   number of copies

RETURN   begins printing the worksheet

To print only a portion of your worksheet, in compressed font,

Place your cursor on the first cell of the block you wish to print and, if you do not see Command List 1 displayed, press:

Esc 1   displays Command List 1

P	starts PRINT command
T	selects Text option
B	selects Block option

Move your cursor to the last cell of the block you wish to print, and press:

RETURN	accepts the specified area for printing
P	selects Printer option
C	selects Compressed (font) option
1	number of copies
RETURN	prints the specified area

EXERCISE 7
AMORTIZATION SCHEDULE SPREADSHEET

DESCRIPTION

Among its many functions, Smart Spreadsheet has two
extremely powerful ones, the PMT and the PRINCIPAL
functions, which allow you to calculate the unknown
payment or the principal of a loan.

To demonstrate this, an amortization schedule has been set
up which can determine either the unknown payment or the
principal.

A report is then generated which contains the principal,
principal payment, interest payment, the principal to date,
and the interest to date for the length of the term.

OPERATIONS PERFORMED

Setting Up the Worksheet Format

Entering Mathematical Formulas

Making Worksheet Entries
(Finding the Unknown Principal from a Known Payment)

Making Worksheet Entries
(Finding the Unknown Payment from a Known Principal)

Saving the Worksheet

Printing the Workheet

FUNCTIONS

@IF
MAX
PMT
PRINCIPAL

COMMANDS

BLANK
COPY
JUSTIFY
PRINT
REFORMAT
SAVE
WIDTH

SETTING UP THE WORKSHEET FORMAT

To set up your Amortization Schedule, use the following directions, copying Figure 1 exactly as illustrated, retaining exact row and column locations of all information.

When Smart Spreadsheet is first loaded into the computer, the columns widths are 10 characters (the default).

All the column widths in this worksheet need to be expanded, except for Column 1.

Place your cursor on Column 2 and press:

Esc	displays Command List 1
3	displays Command List 3
W	starts WIDTH command
14	width of column
RETURN	enters width
C	selects Columns option

Move your cursor to Column 6, last column to widen, and press:

RETURN	executes the command

```
                1          2          3          4          5          6
 1   PMT Known
 2   Int Per Year
 3   Term
 4   No. Periods/Yr
 5   PRN Known
 6   ------------------------
 7   PMT Unknown
 8   PRN Unknown
 9
10
11   Term       Principal  Principal  Interest   Principal  Interest
12                         Payment    Payment    To Date    To Date
13   ------------------------------------------------------------------------
```

Figure 1

USING THE FOLLOWING DIRECTIONS, enter the labels in Rows 1 through 8, and in Rows 11 and 12, as illustrated in Figure 1.

Place your cursor on R1C1 and press:

Esc   returns to Enter mode

PMT Known   label to be entered

Press the down cursor key once, which will enter the label and move the cursor to R2C1. Continue typing in the labels illustrated in Figure 1.

The next operation is to center the labels in Rows 11 and 12.

Place your cursor on R11C1, and press:

Esc 3   displays Command List 3
                                      Note: If Command List 3 is already
                                      displayed, you need not press 3.

J   starts JUSTIFY command

C   selects Center option

B   selects Block option

Move your cursor to R12C6. Notice the screen reverses to indicate the area being centered. Press:

RETURN   centers the labels

To enter the dashed line in Row 6, into Columns 1 and 2,

Place your cursor on R6C1 and press:

Esc   returns to Enter mode

\   (backslash) starts Repeat
                                      label, and displays a dashed line

RETURN   enters the dashed line

Next copy the dashed line across the row into Column 2.

Leave your cursor on R6C1 and press:

Esc 1	displays Command List 1
C	starts COPY command
R	selects Right option
S	selects Single-Cell option
1	number of copies
RETURN	copies dashed line across the row into Column 2

Now copy the dashed line down into Row 13.

Leave your cursor on R6C1 and press:

C	starts COPY command
F	selects From option

Move your cursor to R6C2. The screen reverses to indicate the area being copied.

RETURN	enters area to be copied

Move your cursor to R13C1, first cell to copy into, and press:

.	ellipsis, indicates from-to

Move your cursor to R13C6, last cell to copy to, and press:

RETURN	copies dashed line across the row into Column 6

Your worksheet should now look like Figure 1.

ENTERING MATHEMATICAL FORMULAS

You will now begin entering mathematical formulas that will establish the relationship between column and row locations. The formulas and their locations are illustrated in Figure 2.

Smart Spreadsheet is designed to do one of two things with cells when they are copied. The cells are either relative to their new location, or they are absolute, which means they remain the same.

A cell address remains relative if the cell location is either typed in, or if the cursor movement method is used.

To make a cell address absolute, when using the cursor movement method of entering the cell reference, do the following: When your cursor is on the cell you wish to make absolute, press the F3 function key to make the cell reference absolute. The program will automatically insert brackets [ ] around the column and row numbers. The F3 function key is a toggle switch. If you press it again, the cell reference will become relative again. If you wish, you may *type* the brackets around the column and row numbers. Example: r[3]c[1].

Making cell references absolute is demonstrated in some of the formulas below, which you are about to enter.

Formula one, to the right of PMT Unknown (Payment Unknown), calculates the unknown payment.

Place your cursor on R7C3 and press:

Esc   returns to Edit mode

=   displays Enter formula:

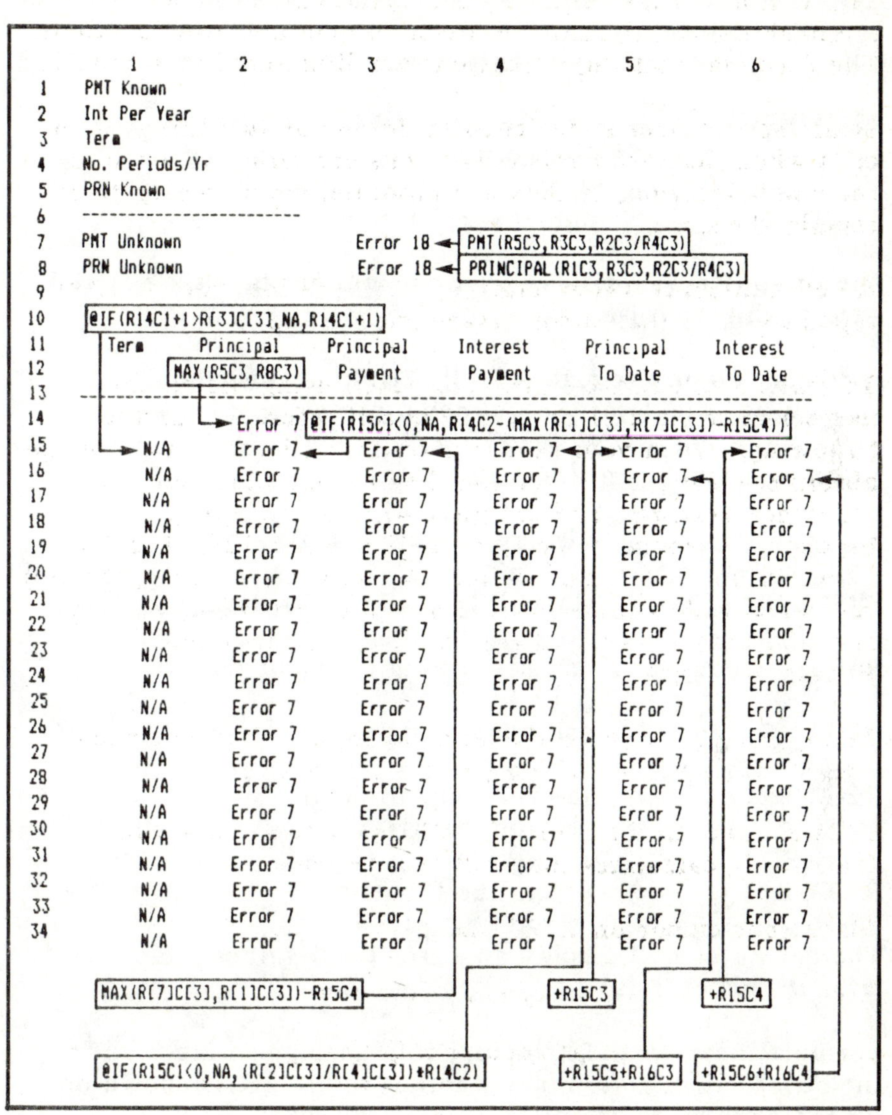

Figure 2

PMT(starts PAYMENT function

R5C3,   cell containing Principal Known

R3C3,   cell containing Term

R2C3/R4C3)   Int Per Year divided by
                        No. Periods/Yr

RETURN   enters the formula

The computer will display an Error until values are entered
later in this exercise.

Formula two, to the right of PRN Unknown (Principal
Unknown), calculates the unknown principal.

Place your cursor on R8C3 and press:

=   displays Enter formula:

PRINCIPAL(starts PRINCIPAL function

R1C3,   cell containing Payment Known

R3C3,   cell containing Term

R2C3/R4C3)   Int Per Year divided
                        by No. Periods/Yr

RETURN   enters the formula

The computer will display an Error until values are entered
later in this exercise.

Formula three, in the Principal column, immediately under
the dashed line, determines whether to use PRN Known or
PRN Unknown as the principal for the loan.

Place your cursor on R14C2 and type:

=   displays Enter formula:

MAX(	selects maximum value in the following list
R5C3,	cell containing PRN Known
R8C3)	cell containing PRN Unknown
RETURN	enters the formula

The computer will display Error until values are entered
later in this exercise.

Formula four, in the Term column, determines the Term.

Place your cursor on R15C1 and type:

| = | displays Enter formula: |
| @IF(| starts IF function |

Move your cursor to R14C1, previous term, and type:

+	adds
1	value to be added
>	greater than, logical operator to compare against

Move your cursor to R3C3, cell containing Term, and press
the F3 function key. The program automatically inserts
brackets [ ] around the row and column numbers and makes
the cell reference *absolute*. Now type:

| , | comma, separates expressions |
| NA, | selected if comparison is true |

Move your cursor to R14C1 and type:

| + | adds |
| 1 | value to be added |

)   closes expression

RETURN   enters the formula

The computer will display N/A until values are entered later in this exercise.

Formula five, in the Principal column, calculates the principal minus principal payment.

Place your cursor on R15C2 and type:

=   displays Enter formula:

@IF(starts IF function

R15C1   cell containing Term

<   less than, logical operator
                               to compare against

0,   zero, value to compare against

NA,   selected if comparison is true

R14C2   previous principal

-                               subtracts

(MAX(selects maximum value in
                               the following list

Move your cursor to R1C3, cell containing PMT Known, and press the F3 function key. The program automatically inserts brackets [ ] around the row and column numbers and makes the cell reference *absolute*. Now type:

,   comma, separates expressions

Move your cursor to R7C3, cell containing PMT Unknown, and press the F3 function key. The program automatically inserts brackets [ ] around the row and column numbers and makes the cell reference *absolute*. Now type:

)   right parenthesis, closes
                           expression

-                          subtracts

R15C4   cell containing Interest
                           Payment. The value generated from
                           this formula is selected if the
                           comparison is false.

))   closes expressions

RETURN   enters the formula

The computer will display Error until values are entered
later in this exercise.

Formula six, in the Principal Payment column, determines
the payment made toward the principal.

Place your cursor on R15C3 and type:

=   displays Enter formula:

MAX(selects maximum value in
                           the following list

Move your cursor to R7C3, cell containing PMT Unknown,
and press the F3 function key. The program automatically
inserts brackets [ ] around the row and column numbers and
makes the cell reference *absolute*. Now type:

,   comma, separates expressions

Move your cursor to R1C3, cell containing PMT Known, and
press the F3 function key. The program automatically inserts
brackets [ ] around the row and column numbers and makes
the cell reference *absolute*. Now type:

)   right parenthesis, closes
                           expression

-                          subtracts

R15C4   cell containing Interest Payment

RETURN   enters the formula

Computer displays Error until values are entered later in this exercise.

Formula seven, in the Interest Payment column, calculates the interest payment against the principal.

Place your cursor on R15C4 and type:

=   displays Enter formula:

@IF(starts IF function

R15C1   cell containing Term

<   less than, logical operator
                               to compare against

0,   zero, value to compare against

NA,   selected if comparison is true
                               Note: The value from the following
                               formula is selected if the comparison is
                               false.

(left parenthesis, opens
                               expression

Move your cursor to R2C3, Int per Year, and press the F3 function key. The program automatically inserts brackets [ ] around the row and column numbers and makes the cell reference *absolute*. Now type:

/   divides

Move your cursor to R4C3, No. Periods/Yr, and press the F3 function key. The program automatically inserts brackets [ ] around the row and column numbers and makes the cell reference *absolute*. Now type:

)	right parenthesis, closes expression
*	multiplies
R14C2	cell containing previous principal
)	right parenthesis, closes expression
RETURN	enters the formula

The computer will display Error until values are entered later in this exercise.

Formula eight, in the Principal To Date column, picks up the first principal payment and places it in the Principal To date column.

Place your cursor on R15C5 and type:

=	displays Enter formula:
R15C3	first principal payment
RETURN	enters the formula

Computer displays Error until values are entered later in this exercise.

Formula nine in the Principal To Date column, adds the previous Principal To Date amount to the new Principal Payment.

Place your cursor on R16C5 and type:

=	displays Enter formula:
R15C5	cell containing previous Principal to Date
+	adds

R16C3	cell containing new Principal Payment
RETURN	enters the formula

Computer displays Error until values are entered later in this exercise.

Formula ten, in the Interest To Date column, picks up the first Interest Payment and displays it in the Interest To Date column.

Place your cursor on R15C6 and type:

=	displays Enter formula:
R15C4	cell containing first Interest Payment
RETURN	enters the formula

Computer displays Error until values are entered later in this exercise.

Formula eleven, in the Interest To Date column, adds the prior Interest To Date to the new Interest Payment to display the accumulated Interest To Date amounts.

Place your cursor on R16C6 and type:

=	displays Enter formula:
R15C6	prior Interest To Date
+	adds
R16C4	new interest payment
RETURN	executes the command

Computer displays Error until values are entered later in this exercise.

Next you will format the cell in the Term column so that
later it will also be displayed as an integer.

Place your cursor on R15C1 and press:

Esc 3	displays Command List 3
R	starts REFORMAT command
B	selects Block option
RETURN	displays options
N	selects Numeric option
N	selects Normal option
N	selects Nocommas option
0	zero, number of decimals
RETURN	executes the command and formats the selected cell as an integer

The next operation will be to copy the formulas down their
respective columns.

For this exercise you will copy the formulas down through
Row 34, which will allow for 20 payments. However, later,
for your own personal use, you may copy the formulas down
as far as you like.

The first group of formulas to copy will be the Term
through Interest Payment formulas.

Leave your cursor on R15C1 and press:

1	places you in Command List 1
C	starts COPY command
F	selects From option

Move your cursor to R15C4. The screen reverses to indicate the area being copied.

RETURN   enters area to be copied

Move your cursor to R16C1, first cell to copy to, and press the F2 function key (Drop anchor).

Now move your cursor to R34C4, last cell to copy to. The screen reverses to indicate the area being copied to. Press:

RETURN   copies formulas down the
          columns

The next group of formulas to copy will be the Principal To Date and Interest To Date formulas in *Row 16*.

Place your cursor on R16C5 and type:

C   starts COPY command

F   selects From option

Move your cursor to R16C6. The screen reverses to indicate the area being copied.

RETURN   enters area to be copied

Move your cursor to R17C5, first cell to copy to, and press the F2 function key (Drop anchor).

Now move your cursor to R34C6, last cell to copy to. The screen reverses to indicate the area being copied to. Press:

RETURN   copies formulas down the
          columns

Your worksheet should now look like Figure 2.

MAKING WORKSHEET ENTRIES
(Finding the Unknown Principal from a Known Payment)

Using the following instructions, you will now make the
worksheet entries, to find the unknown principal, as
illustrated in Figure 3.

Press the Home key to place your cursor at the top of the
screen.

Place your cursor on R1C3 and type:

Esc   returns to Edit mode

151.47   PMT Known (Payment Known)

RETURN   enters the value

Continue entering the values in Rows 2, 3, 4 and 5, which
are illustrated in Figure 3.

The next operation is to format the cells containing the Term
and the No. Periods/Yr so that the values will be displayed
as integers.

Place your cursor on R3C3 and press:

Esc   returns to Command Menu

3   selects Command Menu 3

R   starts REFORMAT command

B   selects Block option

Move your cursor to R4C3 and press:

RETURN   displays options

N   selects Numeric option

N   selects Normal option

N   selects Nocommas option

	1	2	3	4	5	6
1	PMT Known		151.47			
2	Int Per Year		0.12			
3	Term		20			
4	No. Periods/Yr		12			
5	PRN Known		0.00			
6	-----------------------					
7	PMT Unknown		0.00			
8	PRN Unknown		2,733.36			
9						
10						
11	Term	Principal	Principal	Interest	Principal	Interest
12			Payment	Payment	To Date	To Date
13						
14		2,733.36				
15	1	2,609.22	124.14	27.33	124.14	27.33
16	2	2,483.85	125.38	26.09	249.51	53.43
17	3	2,357.21	126.63	24.84	376.15	78.26
18	4	2,229.32	127.90	23.57	504.04	101.84
19	5	2,100.14	129.18	22.29	633.22	124.13
20	6	1,969.67	130.47	21.00	763.69	145.13
21	7	1,837.90	131.77	19.70	895.46	164.83
22	8	1,704.81	133.09	18.38	1,028.55	183.21
23	9	1,570.38	134.42	17.05	1,162.98	200.25
24	10	1,434.62	135.77	15.70	1,298.74	215.96
25	11	1,297.49	137.12	14.35	1,435.87	230.30
26	12	1,159.00	138.50	12.97	1,574.36	243.28
27	13	1,019.12	139.88	11.59	1,714.24	254.87
28	14	877.84	141.28	10.19	1,855.52	265.06
29	15	735.15	142.69	8.78	1,998.21	273.84
30	16	591.03	144.12	7.35	2,142.33	281.19
31	17	445.47	145.56	5.91	2,287.89	287.10
32	18	298.46	147.02	4.45	2,434.90	291.56
33	19	149.97	148.49	2.98	2,583.39	294.54
34	20	-0.00	149.97	1.50	2,733.36	296.04

Figure 3

0   zero, number of decimals

RETURN   executes the command and
                           formats the selected block
                           as integers

Now that the values are entered, you will have to recalculate
your worksheet.

Press the **F5 function key** to recalculate the worksheet.

Your worksheet should now look like Figure 3.

MAKING WORKSHEET ENTRIES
(Finding the Unknown Payment from a Known Principal)

To demonstrate how to find an unknown payment from a
known principal, as illustrated in Figure 4, you must first
erase the *PMT Known in Row 1*. To do this,

Place your cursor on R1C3, and press:

1   displays Command Menu 1

B   starts BLANK command

B   selects Block option

RETURN   executes the command and
                           blanks the selected cell

Now you will have to recalculate your worksheet to
eliminate the PRN Unknown value in R8C3. Press:

F5 function key   recalculates the worksheet

You may change the values in Rows 2, 3 and 4, the Int Per
Year, Term and No. Periods/Yr. However, for this exercise
we have left them as is.

	1	2	3	4	5	6
1	PMT Known					
2	Int Per Year		0.12			
3	Term		20			
4	No. Periods/Yr		12			
5	PRN Known		2,733.36			
6	-----------------------		------			
7	PMT Unknown		151.47			
8	PRN Unknown		0.00			
9						
10						
11	Term	Principal	Principal	Interest	Principal	Interest
12			Payment	Payment	To Date	To Date
13		-----------	--------	--------	--------	--------
14		2,733.36				
15	1	2,609.22	124.14	27.33	124.14	27.33
16	2	2,483.85	125.38	26.09	249.51	53.43
17	3	2,357.21	126.63	24.84	376.15	78.26
18	4	2,229.32	127.90	23.57	504.04	101.84
19	5	2,100.14	129.18	22.29	633.22	124.13
20	6	1,969.67	130.47	21.00	763.69	145.13
21	7	1,837.90	131.77	19.70	895.46	164.83
22	8	1,704.81	133.09	18.38	1,028.55	183.21
23	9	1,570.38	134.42	17.05	1,162.98	200.25
24	10	1,434.62	135.77	15.70	1,298.74	215.96
25	11	1,297.49	137.12	14.35	1,435.87	230.30
26	12	1,159.00	138.50	12.97	1,574.36	243.28
27	13	1,019.12	139.88	11.59	1,714.24	254.87
28	14	877.84	141.28	10.19	1,855.52	265.06
29	15	735.15	142.69	8.78	1,998.21	273.84
30	16	591.03	144.12	7.35	2,142.33	281.19
31	17	445.47	145.56	5.91	2,287.89	287.10
32	18	298.46	147.02	4.45	2,434.90	291.56
33	19	149.97	148.49	2.98	2,583.39	294.54
34	20	-0.00	149.97	1.50	2,733.36	296.04

Figure 4

To enter the PRN Known amount,

Place your cursor on R5C3, *to the right of PRN Known,* and press:

Esc	returns to Enter mode
2733.36	PRN Known
RETURN	enters the value

You will have to recalculate your worksheet. Press:

F5 function key	recalculates the worksheet

Your worksheet should now look like Figure 4.

SAVING THE WORKSHEET

To save your worksheet, press:

Esc 4	displays Command List 4
S	starts SAVE command and displays Enter worksheet name:
AMORT	filename
RETURN	saves the worksheet

If the worksheet was previously saved under the same name, the message **Overwrite existing file (y/n)** will be displayed. In response, type **Y** to save the worksheet in place of the existing one; or type **N** to save the worksheet under another name, and then follow the prompts.

PRINTING THE WORKSHEET

To print the entire worksheet, in compressed font,

Place your cursor on R1C1 and press:

1	displays Command List 1
P	starts PRINT command
T	selects Text option
W	selects Worksheet option
P	selects Printer option
C	selects Compressed (font) option
1	number of copies
RETURN	begins printing the worksheet

To print only a portion of your worksheet,

Place your cursor on the first cell of the block you wish to print, and press:

P	starts PRINT command
T	selects Text option
B	selects Block option

Move your cursor to the last cell of the block you wish to print, and press:

RETURN	accepts the specified area for printing
P	selects Printer option
C	selects Compressed (font) option
1	number of copies
RETURN	prints the specified area

EXERCISE 8
BUDGET CONSOLIDATION SPREADSHEET

DESCRIPTION

This exercise is about a company that has two offices. Each office maintains its own separate budget; however, a total consolidated budget is needed to determine the overall budget for the company.

This exercise contains 3 worksheets. The first worksheet contains the budget for Office 1; the second worksheet contains the budget for Office 2; the third worksheet is used to consolidate the two separate budgets.

OPERATIONS PERFORMED

Setting Up the Worksheet for Office 1

Entering Mathematical Formulas

Naming Cells

Setting Up the Worksheet for Office 2

Making Worksheet Entries for Office 2

Making Worksheet Entries for Office 1

Setting Up the Consolidated Worksheet

Entering Mathematical Formulas in the Consolidated Worksheet

Consolidating the Two Worksheets

Updating

Saving

Printing

FUNCTIONS

SUM

COMMANDS

ACTIVATE
COPY
JUSTIFY
LOAD
NAME
PRINT
SAVE
UNLOAD
VCOPY
WIDTH

SETTING UP THE WORKSHEET FOR OFFICE 1

Using the following directions, set up the worksheet for
Office 1 by copying Figure 1 exactly as it is illustrated,
retaining exact row and column locations of all information.

When Smart Spreadsheet is first loaded into the computer,
the columns widths are 10 characters (the default).

Column 1 needs to be expanded so that it will be 20
characters wide, in order to accommodate the long labels.

Place your cursor on Column 1 and press:

Esc	displays Command List 1
3	displays Command List 3
W	starts WIDTH command
20	width of column
RETURN	enters width
C	selects Columns option

```
                  1              2           3           4           5
 1    OFFICE 1 EXPENSES    1ST QUARTER
 2    ---------------------------------
 3        DESCRIPTION       JAN 1985    FEB 1985   MARCH 1985    TOTAL
 4    ------------------------------------------------------------------
 5    Rent
 6    Auto
 7    Telephone
 8    Payroll
 9    Supplies
10    Miscellaneous
11    ==================================================================
12    Totals
13
14
15                        2ND QUARTER
16
17        DESCRIPTION      APRIL 1985   MAY 1985    JUNE 1985    TOTAL
18    ------------------------------------------------------------------
19    Rent
20    Auto
21    Telephone
22    Payroll
23    Supplies
24    Miscellaneous
25    ==================================================================
26    Totals
27
28         SUMMARY         1ST MONTH   2ND MONTH   3RD MONTH     TOTAL
29    ------------------------------------------------------------------
30     1ST QUARTER
31     2ND QUARTER
32    ==================================================================
33    TOTALS
```

Figure 1

1	number of columns to widen
RETURN	executes the command

The remaining columns need to be expanded so that they will be 12 characters wide.

Place your cursor on Column 2 and press:

W	starts WIDTH command
12	width of column
RETURN	enters width
C	selects Columns option
4	number of columns to widen
RETURN	executes the command

The next operation is to type in the row and column labels.

Place your cursor on R1C1 and press:

Esc	returns to Enter mode
OFFICE 1 EXPENSES	label to be entered

Press the right cursor key once, which will enter the label and move the cursor to R1C2.

Type:

"	double quotation mark, prepares cell for text information
1ST QUARTER	label to be entered

Using the cursor keys, place your cursor on R3C1 and continue typing in the labels illustrated in Figure 1.

NOTE

When entering text which begins with a number (1ST QUARTER), it is necessary to type a double quotation mark (") first. This tells the computer that the number is to be considered as text, instead of as a value.

Labels which require a double quotation mark before entering are on Rows 15, 28, 30 and 31.

After the labels are typed in, the next operation is to center the labels in Rows 3, 17 and 28.

Place your cursor on R3C1, first cell to be centered, and press:

Esc 3	displays Command List 3 Note: If Command List 3 is already displayed, you need not press 3.
J	starts JUSTIFY command
C	selects Center option
R	selects Row option
RETURN	centers the labels

Place your cursor on R17C1 and repeat the above procedure to center the labels in Rows 17. Then center the labels in Row 28.

Next we will place a dashed line across Row 2.

Place your cursor on R2C1 and press:

Esc	returns to Enter mode
\	backslash, starts repeat label and displays a dashed line
RETURN	enters the dashed line

Now copy the dashed line across the row into Column 2, using the COPY command.

Leave your cursor on R2C1 and press:

Esc 1   displays Command List 1

C   starts COPY command

R   selects Right option

S   selects Single-Cell option

1   number of copies

RETURN   copies dashed line across
                        the row into Column 2

Now you will copy the dashed line down into Row 4.

Leave your cursor on R2C1 and press:

C   starts COPY command

F   selects From option

RETURN   enters area to be copied

Move your cursor to R4C1, first cell to copy into.

Press the F2 (drop anchor) function key.

Move your cursor to R4C5 and press:

RETURN   copies dashed line across
                        Row 4 into Column 5

To copy the dashed line in Row 4 down into Row 18,

Place your cursor on R4C1 and press:

C   starts COPY command

F   selects From option

Move your cursor to R4C5 and press:

RETURN   enters area to be copied

Move your cursor to R18C1, cell to copy to, and press:

RETURN   copies the dashed line into Row 18

To copy the dashed line into Row 29, repeat the above copy procedure, substituting R29C1 as the cell to copy to.

To enter the double-dashed line in Row 11,

Place your cursor on R11C1 and press:

Esc   returns to Enter mode

\   backslash, starts repeat label

=   equal sign, label to be repeated

RETURN   enters the double-dashed line

To copy the double-dashed across the row into the remaining columns,

Leave your cursor on R11C1 and press:

Esc   displays Command List 1

C   starts COPY command

R   selects Right option

S   selects Single-Cell option

4   number of copies

RETURN   executes the command

Now copy the double-dashed line into Row 25.

Leave your cursor on R11C1 and type:

C   starts COPY command

F   selects From option

Move your cursor to R11C5 and press:

RETURN   accepts area to be copied

Move your cursor to R25C1 and press:

RETURN   executes the command

Use the above procedure to copy the double-dashed line down into Row 32.

When all the labels, dashed and double-dashed lines have been entered, your worksheet should look like Figure 1.

ENTERING MATHEMATICAL FORMULAS

Using the following directions, you will now enter mathematical formulas that will establish the relationship between column and row positions. The formulas and their locations are illustrated in Figure 2.

Formula one, in the 1st Quarter TOTAL column, adds the values in the January, February and March columns.

1   2   3   4   5
1   OFFICE 1 EXPENSES   1ST QUARTER
2   --------------------------------
3   DESCRIPTION   JAN 1985   FEB 1985   MARCH 1985   TOTAL
4   ---
5   Rent   SUM(R5C2:R5C4)   0.00
6   Auto   0.00
7   Telephone   0.00
8   Payroll   0.00
9   Supplies   SUM(R5C2:R10C2)   0.00
10 Miscellaneous   0.00
11 ===
12 Totals   0.00   0.00   0.00   0.00
13
14
15   2ND QUARTER
16
17   DESCRIPTION   APRIL 1985   MAY 1985   JUNE 1985   TOTAL
18 ---
19 Rent   0.00
20 Auto   0.00
21 Telephone   0.00
22 Payroll   0.00
23 Supplies   0.00
24 Miscellaneous   0.00
25 ===
26 Totals   0.00   0.00   0.00   0.00
27
28   SUMMARY   1ST MONTH   2ND MONTH   3RD MONTH   TOTAL
29 ---
30   1ST QUARTER   0.00   0.00   0.00   0.00
31   2ND QUARTER   0.00   0.00   0.00   0.00
32 ===
33 TOTALS   0.00   0.00   0.00   0.00

R12C2

R26C2   SUM(R30C2:R31C2)

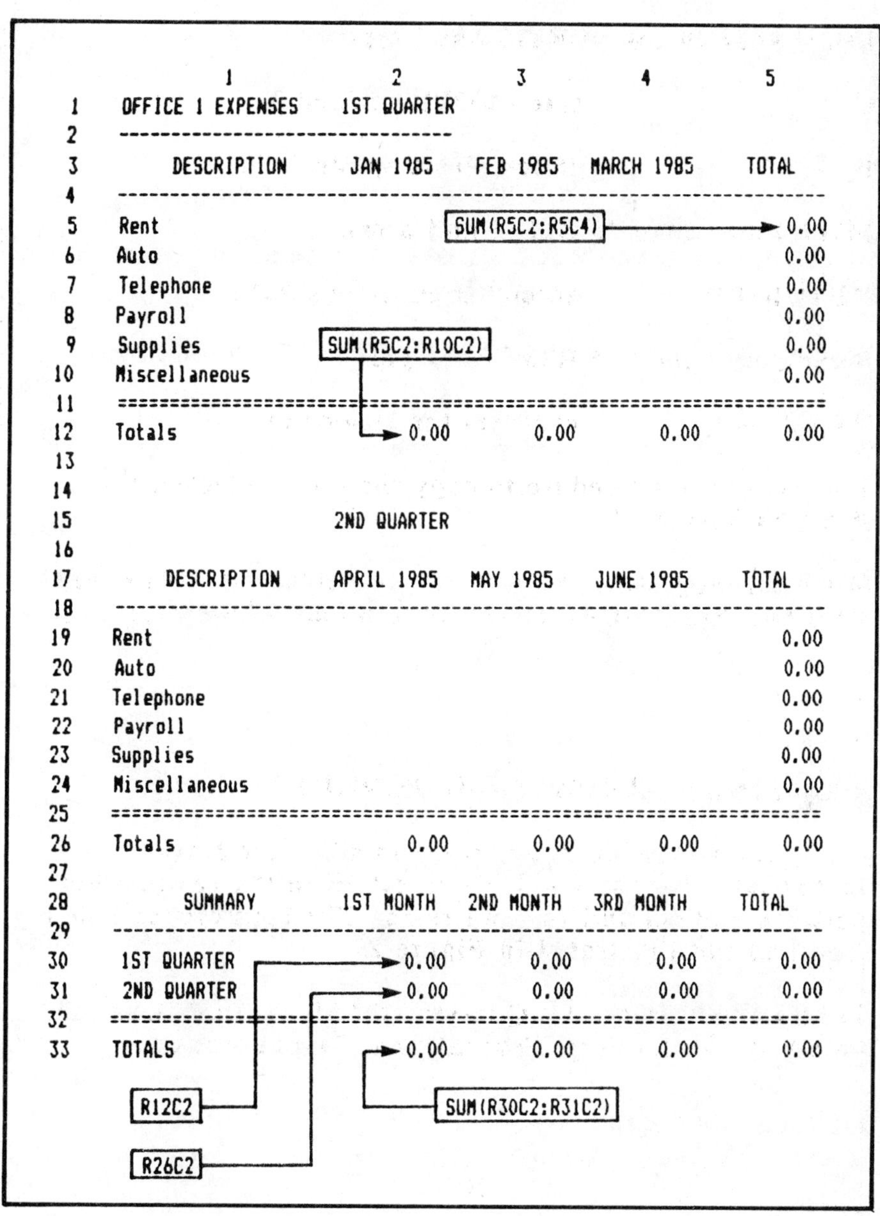

Figure 2

Place your cursor on R5C5 and press:

Esc	returns to Enter mode
=	displays Enter formula:
SUM(	starts SUM function, which adds values in the following list

Move your cursor to R5C2, Jan 1985 column, and press the **F2 (Drop Anchor) function key.**

Now move your cursor to R5C4, March 1985 column, and type:

)	right parenthesis, closes list
RETURN	enters the formula

The next operation is to copy the formula just entered down the column between the single and double-dashed lines.

Leave your cursor on R5C5 and press:

Esc 1	displays Command List 1
C	starts COPY command
D	selects Down option
S	selects Single-Cell option
5	number of copies
RETURN	executes the command

Formula two, in the 1st Quarter, Totals row, adds the values in the JAN 1985 column.

Place your cursor on R12C2 and press:

Esc	returns to Enter mode
=	displays Enter formula:

SUM(starts SUM function, which
                        adds values in the following list

Move your cursor to R5C2, first cell in list to add, and press
the **F2 (Drop Anchor) function key.**

Now move your cursor to R10C2, last cell in list to add, and
type:

)   right parenthesis, closes list

RETURN   enters the formula

The next operation is to copy the formula just entered across
the row into the FEB 1985, MARCH 1985 and TOTAL
columns.

Leave your cursor on R12C2 and press:

Esc 1   displays Command List 1

C   starts COPY command

R   selects Right option

S   selects Single-Cell option

3   number of copies

RETURN   executes the command

The next operation will be to copy the formulas just entered
in 1st Quarter into the 2nd Quarter (April, May and June).

Place your cursor on R5C2 and type:

C   starts COPY command

F   selects From option

Move your cursor to R12C5, last cell to copy. The screen
reverses to indicate the area being copied.

RETURN   enters area to be copied

Move your cursor to R19C2, first cell to copy into, and press:

RETURN   executes the command

Formula three, in the SUMMARY section, in the 1st Quarter
row, picks up the value in the 1st Quarter, Jan 1985 column,
Totals row, and displays it in the Summary section.

Place your cursor on R30C2 and press:

Esc   returns to Enter mode

=   displays Enter formula:

R12C2   1st Quarter, Jan, Totals value

RETURN   enters the formula

Formula four, in the SUMMARY section, in the 2nd Quarter
row, picks up the value in the 2nd Quarter, April 1985
column, Totals row, and displays it in the Summary section.

Place your cursor on R31C2 and press:

=   displays Enter formula:

R26C2   2nd Quarter, April, Totals value

RETURN   enters the formula

Next you will copy the two formulas just entered across their
respective rows.

Place your cursor on R30C2 and press:

Esc 1   displays Command List 1

C   starts COPY command

F   selects From option

Move your cursor to R31C2, last cell to copy. The screen
reverses to indicate the area being copied.

RETURN   enters area to be copied

Move your cursor to R30C3, first cell to copy into, and press
the **F2 (Drop Anchor) function key.**

Move your cursor to R31C5, last cell to copy into, and press:

RETURN   executes the command

Formula five, in the Summary section, adds the 1st Quarter
and 2nd Quarter TOTALS for the 1st Month.

Place your cursor on R33C2 and press:

Esc   returns to Enter mode

=   displays Enter formula:

SUM(starts SUM function, which
                        adds values in the following list

Move your cursor to R30C2 and press the **F2 (Drop Anchor)
function key.**

Move your cursor to R31C2 and type:

)   right parenthesis, closes the list

RETURN   enters the formula

The next operation is to copy the formula just entered across
the TOTALS row, into the remaining columns.

Leave your cursor on R33C2 and press:

Esc 1   displays Command List 1

C   starts COPY command

R   selects Right option

S	selects Single-Cell option
3	number of copies
RETURN	executes the command

Your worksheet should now look like Figure 2.

NAMING CELLS

You will now name two groups of cells so that they can be easily used, later in this exercise, when the budget consolidation takes place.

The first group of cells to name is in the Summary section, 1st Quarter row.

Place your cursor on R30C2 and, assuming Command List 1 is still displayed, press:

N	starts NAME command
D	selects Define option
O1FQ	name of cells (**Office 1 First Quarter**) Note: Be sure to type the **letter O**, and *not* a zero.
RETURN	displays: Enter definition for this name

Move your cursor to R30C5. The screen will reverse to indicate the area being named. Press:

RETURN	executes the command and names the selected cells

The second group of cells to name is in the Summary section,
2nd Quarter row.

Place your cursor on R31C2 and press:

N	starts NAME command

D	selects Define option

O1SQ	name of cells (Office 1 Second Quarter) Note: Be sure to type the **letter O**, and *not* a zero.

RETURN	displays: Enter definition for this name

Move your cursor to R31C5. The screen will reverse to
indicate the area being named. Press:

RETURN	executes the command and names the selected cells

Now you will need to save the worksheet for later use. Press:

4	displays Command List 4

S	starts SAVE command and displays Enter worksheet name:

OFFICE1	filename

RETURN	saves the worksheet

SETTING UP THE WORKSHEET FOR OFFICE 2

The worksheet for Office 2, which is illustrated in Figure 3,
is identical to the worksheet for Office 1, except for one
label and the names of the cells in the 1st QUARTER and
2nd QUARTER rows in the SUMMARY section.

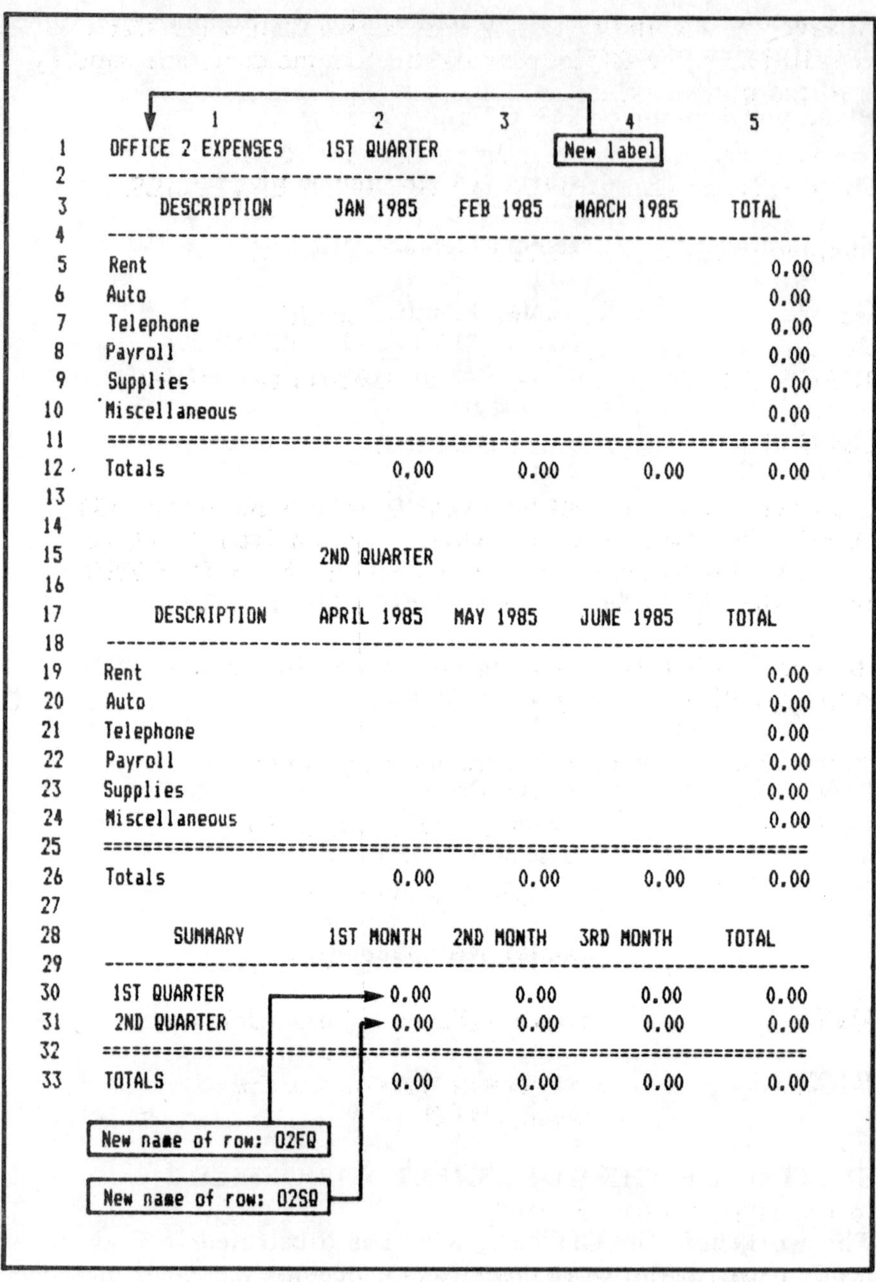


```
                1              2           3           4           5

1   OFFICE 2 EXPENSES   1ST QUARTER               New label
2   -----------------------------------------
3        DESCRIPTION      JAN 1985    FEB 1985   MARCH 1985    TOTAL
4   -----------------------------------------------------------------------
5   Rent                                                        0.00
6   Auto                                                        0.00
7   Telephone                                                   0.00
8   Payroll                                                     0.00
9   Supplies                                                    0.00
10  Miscellaneous                                               0.00
11  =======================================================================
12  Totals                 0.00        0.00        0.00        0.00
13
14
15                       2ND QUARTER
16
17       DESCRIPTION     APRIL 1985   MAY 1985   JUNE 1985     TOTAL
18  -----------------------------------------------------------------------
19  Rent                                                        0.00
20  Auto                                                        0.00
21  Telephone                                                   0.00
22  Payroll                                                     0.00
23  Supplies                                                    0.00
24  Miscellaneous                                               0.00
25  =======================================================================
26  Totals                 0.00        0.00        0.00        0.00
27
28        SUMMARY        1ST MONTH   2ND MONTH   3RD MONTH     TOTAL
29  -----------------------------------------------------------------------
30    1ST QUARTER          0.00        0.00        0.00        0.00
31    2ND QUARTER          0.00        0.00        0.00        0.00
32  =======================================================================
33  TOTALS                 0.00        0.00        0.00        0.00
```


Figure 3

To save time in the setting up of the worksheet for Office 2,
we will leave the Office 1 worksheet in memory, and modify
it where necessary.

The first alteration is to change the label OFFICE 1
EXPENSES so that it will read OFFICE 2 EXPENSES.

Place your cursor on R1C1 and press:

Esc   returns to Enter mode

OFFICE 2 EXPENSES   label to be entered

RETURN   enters the label

The next alteration will be to change the name of the 1ST
QUARTER row in the SUMMARY section from O1FQ to
O2FQ, and then change the name of the 2ND QUARTER
row in the SUMMARY section from O1SQ to O2SQ.

To accomplish this, you must first Undefine (delete) the
names O1FQ and O1SQ.

Leave your cursor on any location and press:

Esc 1   displays Command List 1

N   starts NAME command

U   selects Undefine option

O1FQ   name to be undefined (deleted)

RETURN   Undefines, or deletes, the
                   name O1FQ

To undefine the name O1SQ,

Leave your cursor on any location and type:

N   starts NAME command

U   selects Undefine option

O1SQ	name to be undefined (deleted)
RETURN	Undefines, or deletes, the name O1SQ

The next operation is to rename the cells in the 1ST QUARTER and 2ND QUARTER SUMMARY section (Rows 30 and 31).

First rename the cells in the 1ST QUARTER row, Row 30.

Place your cursor on R30C2 and press:

N	starts NAME command
D	selects Define option
O2FQ	name of cells (Office 2 First Quarter) Note: Be sure to type the letter O, and *not* a zero.
RETURN	displays Enter definition for this name

Move your cursor to R30C5. The screen will reverse to indicate the area being named. Press:

RETURN	executes the command and names the selected cells

The second group of cells to rename is the 2ND QUARTER row, Row 31.

Place your cursor on R31C2 and press:

N	starts NAME command
D	selects Define option

O2SQ   name of cells
                        (Office 2 Second Quarter)
                        Note: Be sure to type the letter **O**, and
                        not a zero.

RETURN   displays
                        Enter definition for this name

Move your cursor to R31C5. The screen will reverse to
indicate the area being named. Press:

RETURN   executes the command and
                        names the selected cells

MAKING WORKSHEET ENTRIES FOR OFFICE 2

Now that the worksheet is complete for Office 2, using the
following directions, make the worksheet entries as
illustrated in Figure 4.

Place your cursor on R5C2 and press:

Esc   returns to Enter mode

Type:

550   value to be entered

Move your cursor to R5C3 and continue making the entries
exactly as illustrated in Figure 4.

NOTE

Make entries only into Columns 2, 3 and 4 between
the single and double-dashed lines.

DO NOT MAKE ENTRIES into Column 5 or into
Rows 12, 26, 30, 31 and 33. These cells contain
formulas, and the formulas will be erased if you make
entries there.

	1	2	3	4	5
1	OFFICE 2 EXPENSES	1ST QUARTER			
2	-----------------------------------				
3	DESCRIPTION	JAN 1985	FEB 1985	MARCH 1985	TOTAL
4	---				
5	Rent	550.00	550.00	550.00	1,650.00
6	Auto	100.00	100.00	100.00	300.00
7	Telephone	300.00	400.00	400.00	1,100.00
8	Payroll	6,500.00	6,500.00	6,500.00	19,500.00
9	Supplies	300.00	300.00	300.00	900.00
10	Miscellaneous	100.00	100.00	100.00	300.00
11	===				
12	Totals	7,850.00	7,950.00	7,950.00	23,750.00
13					
14					
15	2ND QUARTER				
16					
17	DESCRIPTION	APRIL 1985	MAY 1985	JUNE 1985	TOTAL
18	---				
19	Rent	550.00	550.00	550.00	1,650.00
20	Auto	100.00	200.00	200.00	500.00
21	Telephone	300.00	300.00	300.00	900.00
22	Payroll	6,500.00	6,500.00	6,500.00	19,500.00
23	Supplies	200.00	200.00	200.00	600.00
24	Miscellaneous	100.00	100.00	100.00	300.00
25	===				
26	Totals	7,750.00	7,850.00	7,850.00	23,450.00
27					
28	SUMMARY	1ST MONTH	2ND MONTH	3RD MONTH	TOTAL
29	---				
30	1ST QUARTER	7,850.00	7,950.00	7,950.00	23,750.00
31	2ND QUARTER	7,750.00	7,850.00	7,850.00	23,450.00
32	===				
33	TOTALS	15,600.00	15,800.00	15,800.00	47,200.00

Figure 4

After the entries are made, you will need to recalculate your worksheet. Press:

F5 function key   recalculates worksheet

After recalculation, your worksheet should look like Figure 4.

Now the worksheet must be saved. Press:

Esc 4   displays Command List 4

S   starts SAVE command and displays
                 Enter worksheet name:

OFFICE2   filename

RETURN   saves the worksheet

MAKING WORKSHEET ENTRIES FOR OFFICE 1

Now we will need to make entries in the Office 1 worksheet.

First Office 2 worksheet must be cleared from the screen. Press:

U   starts UNLOAD command

If you are prompted for the filename to Unload, type: Office 2.

To load Office 1 back into memory, press:

L   starts LOAD command
                 and displays a list of files

Office1   name of file to be loaded

RETURN   displays Select option:
                 Non-Resident Resident

R   selects Resident option and loads
                         Office 1 worksheet into memory

Press:

Esc   returns to Enter mode

Make your worksheet entries as illustrated in Figure 5.

NOTE

Make entries only into Columns 2, 3 and 4 between
the single and double-dashed lines.

DO NOT MAKE ENTRIES into Column 5 or into
Rows 12, 26, 30, 31 and 33. These cells contain
formulas, and the formulas will be erased if you make
entries there.

After all entries are made, you must recalculate your
worksheet. Press:

F5 function key   recalculates worksheet

Your worksheet should now look like Figure 5.

The next operation is to save the Office 1 worksheet back
onto disk.

Leave your cursor on any location, and press:

Esc 4   displays Command List 4

S   starts SAVE command and displays
                         Enter worksheet name:

OFFICE1   filename

RETURN   saves the worksheet

```
              1              2          3           4           5

 1    OFFICE 1 EXPENSES    1ST QUARTER
 2    --------------------------------
 3       DESCRIPTION       JAN 1985   FEB 1985   MARCH 1985    TOTAL
 4    -------------------------------------------------------------------
 5    Rent                   800.00     800.00      800.00    2,400.00
 6    Auto                   250.00     250.00      275.00      775.00
 7    Telephone               75.00     100.00       75.00      250.00
 8    Payroll              8,000.00   8,000.00    6,000.00   22,000.00
 9    Supplies                75.00      30.00       30.00      135.00
10    Miscellaneous           50.00      50.00       50.00      150.00
11    ===================================================================
12    Totals               9,250.00   9,230.00    7,230.00   25,710.00
13
14
15                        2ND QUARTER
16
17       DESCRIPTION      APRIL 1985   MAY 1985   JUNE 1985     TOTAL
18    -------------------------------------------------------------------
19    Rent                   800.00     800.00      800.00    2,400.00
20    Auto                   250.00     400.00      400.00    1,050.00
21    Telephone               75.00      75.00       75.00      225.00
22    Payroll              6,000.00   6,000.00    6,000.00   18,000.00
23    Supplies                50.00      50.00       50.00      150.00
24    Miscellaneous           50.00      50.00       50.00      150.00
25    ===================================================================
26    Totals               7,225.00   7,375.00    7,375.00   21,975.00
27
28       SUMMARY          1ST MONTH   2ND MONTH   3RD MONTH     TOTAL
29    -------------------------------------------------------------------
30      1ST QUARTER        9,250.00   9,230.00    7,230.00   25,710.00
31      2ND QUARTER        7,225.00   7,375.00    7,375.00   21,975.00
32    ===================================================================
33    TOTALS              16,475.00  16,605.00   14,605.00   47,685.00
```

Figure 5

SETTING UP THE CONSOLIDATED WORKSHEET

Before setting up the consolidated worksheet, which is illustrated in Figure 6, we will first clear memory of the existing worksheet.

Leave your cursor on any location and press:

U   starts UNLOAD command
                            and clears the screen

If you are prompted to type in the filename to be unloaded (cleared from the screen), type: Office1 and press RETURN.

The first operation in setting up the consolidated worksheet is to expand the width of all the columns so that they will be 14 characters wide.

Place your cursor on Column 1 and press:

3   displays Command List 3

W   starts WIDTH command

14   width of column

RETURN   enters width

A   selects All option and expands the
                            width of all columns

Esc   returns to Enter mode

Use the following directions for entering the labels for the consolidated worksheet as illustrated in Figure 6, retaining exact row and column locations of all information.

Place your cursor on R1C1 and type:

CONSOLIDATED BUDGET

```
              1             2             3             4             5
 1   CONSOLIDATED BUDGET

 2

 3   OFFICE 1      1ST MONTH    2ND MONTH    3RD MONTH    TOTAL

 4   ----------------------------------------------------------------------

 5     1ST QTR
 6     2ND QTR

 7   ======================================================================

 8   TOTALS

 9

10

11   OFFICE 2      1ST MONTH    2ND MONTH    3RD MONTH    TOTAL

12   ----------------------------------------------------------------------

13     1ST QTR
14     2ND QTR

15   ======================================================================

16   TOTALS

17

18

19   SUMMARY OF OFFICE 1 AND OFFICE 2

20                 1ST MONTH    2ND MONTH    3RD MONTH    TOTAL

21     1ST QTR
22     2ND QTR

23   ======================================================================

24   TOTALS
```

Figure 6

Now place your cursor on R3C1, and, *after reading the following NOTE*, continue typing in the labels as illustrated in Figure 6.

NOTE

When entering text which begins with a number, such as 1st MONTH, 2ND MONTH, etc., it is necessary to type a double quotation mark (") first. This tells the computer that the number is to be considered as text, instead of as a value. Other labels in this worksheet that begin with numbers are located in Rows 3, 5, 6, 11, 13, 14, 20, 21 and 22.

When the labels have been typed in, a dashed line has to be entered on Row 4.

Place your cursor on R4C1 and press:

\	backslash, displays a dashed line
RETURN	enters the dashed line

To copy the dashed line across the row into the remaining columns,

Leave your cursor on R4C1 and press:

Esc 1	displays Command List 1
C	starts COPY command
R	selects Right option
S	selects Single-Cell option
4	number of copies
RETURN	copies dashed line across the row into Column 5

Now you will copy the dashed line down into Row 12.

Leave your cursor on R4C1 and press:

C	starts COPY command
F	selects From option

Move the cursor to R4C5 and press:

RETURN	enters area to be copied

Move your cursor to R12C1, first cell to copy into, and press:

RETURN	copies dashed line into Row 12

To enter the double-dashed line in Row 7,

Place your cursor on R7C1 and press:

Esc	returns to Enter mode
\	backslash, starts repeat label
=	equal sign, label to be repeated
RETURN	enters the double-dashed line

To copy the double-dashed across the row into the remaining columns,

Leave your cursor on R7C1 and press:

Esc	displays Command List 1
C	starts COPY command
R	selects Right option
S	selects Single-Cell option

4   number of copies

RETURN   executes the command

To copy the double-dashed line into Row 15,

Leave your cursor on R7C1 and type:

C   starts COPY command

F   selects From option

Move your cursor to R7C5 and press:

RETURN   accepts area to be copied

Move your cursor to R15C1 and press:

RETURN   executes the command

Use the above procedure to copy the double-dashed line down into Row 23.

When all the labels and dashed and double-dashed lines have been entered, your consolidated worksheet should look like Figure 6.

ENTERING MATHEMATICAL FORMULAS IN THE CONSOLIDATED WORKSHEET

The formulas and their locations are illustrated in Figure 7.

Formula one, in the OFFICE 1, 1ST MTH, TOTALS row, adds the 1ST and 2ND QUARTERS for the 1ST MONTH, between the single and double-dashed lines.

Place your cursor on R8C2 and press:

Esc   returns to Enter mode

=   displays Enter formula:

1   CONSOLIDATED BUDGET
3   OFFICE 1   1ST MONTH   2ND MONTH   3RD MONTH   TOTAL
5   1ST QTR
6   2ND QTR
8   TOTALS   0.00   0.00   0.00   0.00
9   SUM(R5C2:R6C2)
11   OFFICE 2   1ST MONTH   2ND MONTH   3RD MONTH   TOTAL
13   1ST QTR
14   2ND QTR
16   TOTALS   0.00   0.00   0.00   0.00
19   SUMMARY OF OFFICE 1 AND OFFICE 2
20   1ST MONTH   2ND MONTH   3RD MONTH   TOTAL
21   1ST QTR   0.00   0.00   0.00   0.00
22   2ND QTR   0.00   0.00   0.00   0.00
24   TOTALS   0.00   0.00   0.00   0.00
R5C2+R13C2

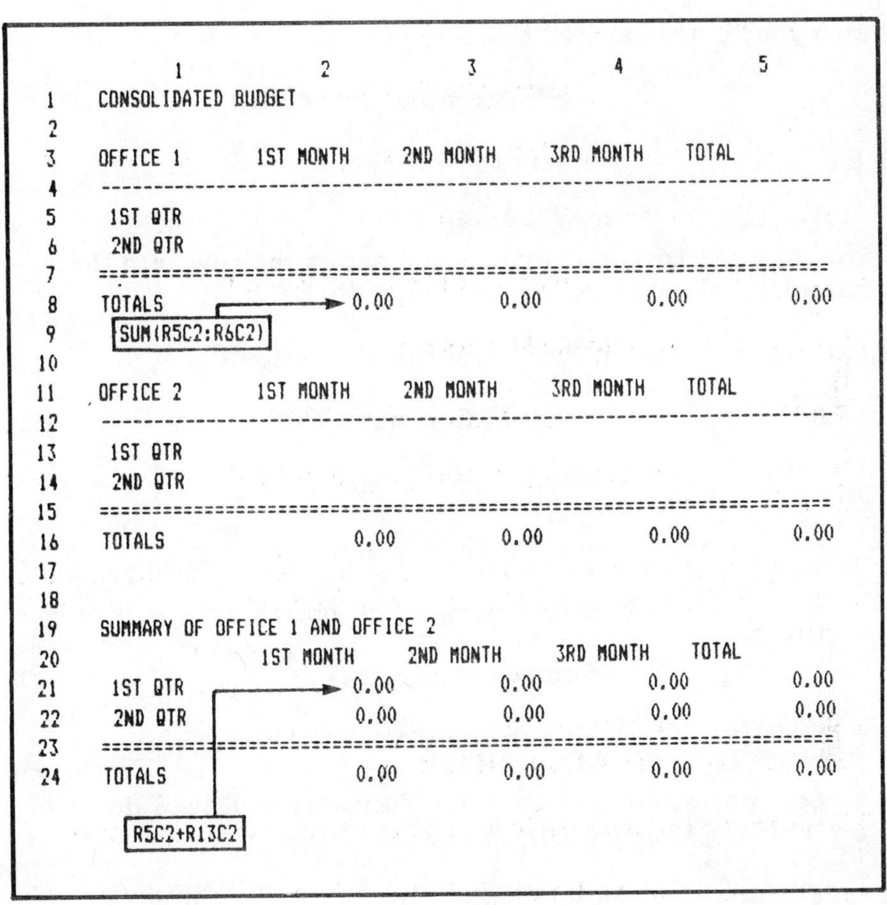

Figure 7

SUM(starts SUM function which
                            adds values in the following list

Move your cursor to R5C2 and press the **F2 (Drop Anchor)**
function key.

Move your cursor to R6C2 and type:

)   right parenthesis, ends list

RETURN   enters the formula

Now copy the formula just entered across the row into the
remaining columns.

Leave your cursor on R8C2 and press:

Esc 1   displays Command List 1

C   starts COPY command

R   selects Right option

S   selects Single-Cell option

3   number of copies

RETURN   executes the command

The next operation is to copy the formulas in Row 8 down to
Row 16, TOTALS row for OFFICE 2.

Leave your cursor on R8C2 and type:

C   starts COPY command

F   selects From option

Move your cursor to R8C5 and press:

RETURN   accepts cells to be copied

Move your cursor to R16C2 and press:

RETURN   executes the command

Next copy the formulas down to Row 24, TOTALS row of the SUMMARY section.

Leave your cursor on R8C2 and type:

C   starts COPY command

F   selects From option

Move your cursor to R8C5 and press:

RETURN   accepts cells to be copied

Move your cursor to R24C2 and press:

RETURN   executes the command

Formula two, in the SUMMARY section, 1ST QTR, 1ST MONTH, adds the value in OFFICE 1, 1ST QTR, for the 1ST MONTH to the value in OFFICE 2, 1ST QTR, for the 1ST MONTH.

Place your cursor on R21C2 and type:

Esc   returns to Enter mode

=   displays Enter Formula:

R5C2   value in OFFICE 1, 1ST QTR, 1ST MTH

+   adds

R13C2   value in OFFICE 2, 1ST QTR, 1ST MTH

RETURN   enters the formula

Next you will copy the formula just entered, across the row into the remaining columns.

Leave your cursor on R21C2 and press:

Esc	displays Command List 1
C	starts COPY command
R	selects Right option
S	selects Single-Cell option
3	number of copies
RETURN	executes the command

Now copy the formulas from Row 21, 1st QTR, into Row 22, 2ND QTR.

Leave your cursor on R21C2 and type:

C	starts COPY command
F	selects From option

Move your cursor to R21C5 and press:

RETURN	accepts cells to be copied

Move your cursor to R22C2 and press:

RETURN	executes the command

Your worksheet should now look like Figure 7.

Save the consolidated worksheet by pressing:

4	displays Command list 4
S	starts SAVE command

CONSOL   filename

RETURN   saves the consolidated worksheet

CONSOLIDATING THE TWO WORKSHEETS

Now that the consolidated worksheet has been set up, we will consolidate the information from Office 1 and Office 2 worksheets into the consolidated worksheet, as illustrated in Figure 8.

The first consolidation operation will be to bring the 1ST QUARTER totals from the Office 1 worksheet and place it in OFFICE 1, 1ST QUARTER row.

To obtain values from the OFFICE 1 worksheet you must first ACTIVATE that worksheet. To do this, press:

4   displays Command List 4

A   starts ACTIVATE command and
                     displays a list of the files.

A prompt appears requesting the name of the worksheet to be activated. Type:

OFFICE1   name of file to Activate

RETURN   displays Select option:
                     Non-Resident Resident

R   selects Resident option

The OFFICE1 worksheet is now available for use.

First the values named O1FQ from the OFFICE1 worksheet need to be copied onto the consolidated worksheet.

Place your cursor on R5C2, first to copy into, and press:

1   displays Command List 1

V   selects VCOPY command

```
         1              2            3            4            5
 1  CONSOLIDATED BUDGET
 2
 3  OFFICE 1       1ST MONTH    2ND MONTH    3RD MONTH    TOTAL
 4  ----------------------------------------------------------------
 5    1ST QTR        9,250.00     9,230.00     7,230.00    25,710.00
 6    2ND QTR        7,225.00     7,375.00     7,375.00    21,975.00
 7  ================================================================
 8  TOTALS          16,475.00    16,605.00    14,605.00    47,685.00
 9
10
11  OFFICE 2       1ST MONTH    2ND MONTH    3RD MONTH    TOTAL
12  ----------------------------------------------------------------
13    1ST QTR        7,850.00     7,950.00     7,950.00    23,750.00
14    2ND QTR        7,750.00     7,850.00     7,850.00    23,450.00
15  ================================================================
16  TOTALS          15,600.00    15,800.00    15,800.00    47,200.00
17
18
19  SUMMARY OF OFFICE 1 AND OFFICE 2
20                 1ST MONTH    2ND MONTH    3RD MONTH    TOTAL
21    1ST QTR       17,100.00    17,180.00    15,180.00    49,460.00
22    2ND QTR       14,975.00    15,225.00    15,225.00    45,425.00
23  ================================================================
24  TOTALS          32,075.00    32,405.00    30,405.00    94,885.00
```

Figure 8

F   selects From option and displays
                                Enter name or block reference:

OFFICE1.O1FQ   name of worksheet and
                                block of values to copy from
                                Note: A period (.) must separate the
                                worksheet name (**OFFICE1**) from the
                                name of the area to copy from (**O1FQ**)

RETURN   accepts area to copy from
                                and requests area to copy to

You need not enter the area to copy to because your cursor is
positioned on the area to copy to (R5C2). Just press:

RETURN   executes the command and
                                copies the specified values from
                                OFFICE 1 worksheet to the area where
                                the cursor is positioned (R5C2)

The second consolidation operation will be to bring the 2ND
QUARTER totals from the OFFICE 1 worksheet and place it
in OFFICE 1, 2ND QUARTER row.

The Office 1 worksheet is already Activated and ready for
use.

Place your cursor on R6C2, first cell to copy to, and press:

V   selects VCOPY command

F   selects From option and displays
                                Enter name or block reference:

OFFICE1.O1SQ   name of worksheet and
                                block of values to copy from
                                Note: A period (.) must separate the
                                worksheet name (**OFFICE1**) from the
                                name of the area to copy from (**O1SQ**)

RETURN   accepts area to copy from
                                and requests area to copy to

You need not enter the area to copy to because your cursor is positioned on the area to copy to (R6C2). Just press:

RETURN   executes the command and
        copies the specified values from
        OFFICE 1 worksheet to the area where
        the cursor is positioned (R6C2)

The consolidated worksheet must now be recalculated. Press:

F5 (Recalc) function key

The next operation is to copy values from the OFFICE 2 worksheet onto the consolidated worksheet.

The OFFICE 2 worksheet must first be ACTIVATED.

Leave your cursor on any location and press:

4   displays Command List 4

A   starts ACTIVATE command, and
        displays a list of the files

A prompt is now displayed requesting the name of the file to be activated. Type:

OFFICE2   name of file to Activate

RETURN   displays Select option:
        Non-Resident Resident

R   selects Resident option

The OFFICE2 worksheet is now available for use.

The values in the 1ST QTR row for OFFICE 2 need to be copied onto the consolidated worksheet.

Place your cursor on R13C2, first cell to copy to, and press:

1   displays Command List 1

V   selects VCOPY command

F   selects From option and displays
                               Enter name or block reference:

OFFICE2.O2FQ   name of worksheet and
                               block of values to copy from
                               Note: A period (.) must separate the
                               worksheet name (**OFFICE2**) from the
                               name of the area to copy from (**O2FQ**)

RETURN   accepts area to copy from
                               and requests area to copy to

You need not enter the area to copy to because the cursor is
positioned on the area to copy to (R13C2). Just press:

RETURN   executes the command and copies the
                               specified values from OFFICE 2
                               worksheet to the place where the cursor
                               is positioned (R13C2)

The next consolidation operation will be to bring the 2ND
QUARTER totals from the OFFICE 2 worksheet and place
them in OFFICE 2, 2ND QUARTER row in the consolidated
worksheet.

The OFFICE 2 worksheet is already Activated and ready for
use.

Place your cursor on R14C2, first cell to copy to, and press:

V   selects VCOPY command

F   selects From option and displays
                               Enter name or block reference:

OFFICE2.O2SQ	name of worksheet and block of values to copy from Note: A period (.) must separate the worksheet name (**OFFICE2**) from the name of the area to copy from (**O2SQ**)
RETURN	accepts area to copy from and requests area to copy to

You need not enter the area to copy to because the cursor is positioned on the area to copy to (R14C2). Just press:

RETURN	executes the command and copies the specified values from OFFICE 2 worksheet to the place where the cursor is positioned (R14C2)

The worksheet must now be recalculated. Press:

F5 (Recalc) function key

Your consolidated worksheet should now look like Figure 8.

UPDATING

To demonstrate how to update a worksheet, we will first save the consolidated worksheet onto disk.

Next OFFICE 1 worksheet will be loaded back into memory, an adjustment will be made to it, and it will then be saved back onto disk.

The consolidated worksheet will be be brought back to memory and updated so that it will reflect the change made to the OFFICE 1 worksheet.

The first operation is to save the consolidated worksheet onto disk.

Leave your cursor on any location and type:

4	displays Command List 4
S	starts SAVE command
CONSOL	filename
RETURN	executes the command

If you see the message: Overwrite existing file (y/n), type Y in response.

The next operation is to load the Office 1 worksheet back into memory.

Leave your cursor on any location and type:

L	starts LOAD command
OFFICE1	name of file to load
RETURN	displays Select option: Non-Resident Resident
R	selects Resident option and loads Office 1 into memory

The adjustment which will be made to Office 1 worksheet will be to add $100 to the amount for Telephone for February, in the 1st Quarter.

Place your cursor on R7C3 and press:

Esc	returns to Enter mode
200	new value to be entered
RETURN	enters the value

You will have to recalculate your worksheet. Press the F5 (Recalc) function key.

Now save the adjusted worksheet. Press:

Esc   displays Command List 4

S   starts SAVE command

OFFICE1   filename

RETURN   executes the command

If you see Overwrite existing file (y/n), press Y in response.

The next operation is to load in the consolidated worksheet.
Press:

L   starts LOAD command

CONSOL   name of file to be loaded

RETURN   displays Select option:
                        Non-Resident Resident

R   selects Resident option
                        and loads worksheet

Now you will have to use the VCOPY command to copy the
new values from OFFICE 1, 1ST QTR expenses, because that
was where the adjustment was made to the February
Telephone expenses.

The Office 1 worksheet is still Activated and ready for use.

Place your cursor on R5C2 and press:

1   displays Command List 1

V   starts VCOPY command

F   selects From option and displays
                        Enter name or block reference:

OFFICE1.O1FQ   name of worksheet and
                           block of values to copy from
                           Note: A period (.) must separate the
                           worksheet name (**OFFICE1**) from the
                           name of the area to copy from (**O1FQ**)

RETURN   accepts area to copy from
                           and requests area to copy to

You do not have to enter the area to copy to because the
cursor is positioned on the area to copy to, R5C2. Just press:

RETURN   executes the command and copies
                           the specified values from Office 1
                           worksheet to the place where the cursor
                           is positioned, R5C2

Last recalculate your consolidated worksheet by pressing the
F5 function key.

Your consolidated worksheet should look like Figure 9.

SAVING

To save your worksheet, press:

Esc 4   displays Command List 4

S   starts SAVE command and displays
                           Enter worksheet name:

CONSOL   filename

RETURN   saves the worksheet

If you see the message Overwrite existing file (y/n)
displayed, respond by typing Y to save the worksheet in
place of the existing one; or type N to save the worksheet
under another name; then follow the prompts.

```
              1             2             3             4             5
 1   CONSOLIDATED BUDGET
 2
 3   OFFICE 1      1ST MONTH    2ND MONTH    3RD MONTH     TOTAL
 4   ----------------------------------------------------------------------
 5     1ST QTR       9,250.00     9,330.00      7,230.00    25,810.00
 6     2ND QTR       7,225.00     7,375.00      7,375.00    21,975.00
 7   ======================================================================
 8   TOTALS         16,475.00    16,705.00     14,605.00    47,785.00
 9
10
11   OFFICE 2      1ST MONTH    2ND MONTH    3RD MONTH     TOTAL
12   ----------------------------------------------------------------------
13     1ST QTR       7,850.00     7,950.00      7,950.00    23,750.00
14     2ND QTR       7,750.00     7,850.00      7,850.00    23,450.00
15   ======================================================================
16   TOTALS         15,600.00    15,800.00     15,800.00    47,200.00
17
18
19   SUMMARY OF OFFICE 1 AND OFFICE 2
20                 1ST MONTH    2ND MONTH    3RD MONTH     TOTAL
21     1ST QTR      17,100.00    17,280.00     15,180.00    49,560.00
22     2ND QTR      14,975.00    15,225.00     15,225.00    45,425.00
23   ======================================================================
24   TOTALS         32,075.00    32,505.00     30,405.00    94,985.00
```

Figure 9

PRINTING

To print the entire worksheet, in compressed font,

Place your cursor on R1C1 and press:

Esc 1	displays Command List 1
P	starts PRINT command
T	selects Text option
B	selects Block option

Move your cursor to the last cell of the block you wish to print, and press:

RETURN	accepts the specified area for printing
P	selects Printer option

To print only a portion of your worksheet, in compressed font,

Place your cursor on the first cell of the block you wish to print, and, if you do not see Command List 1 displayed, press:

Esc 1	displays Command List 1
P	starts PRINT command
T	selects Text option
B	selects Block option

Move your cursor to the last cell of the block you wish to print, and press:

RETURN	accepts the specified area for printing
P	selects Printer option

C   selects Compressed (font) option

1   number of copies

RETURN   prints the specified area

EXERCISE 9
DATABASE, A SALES INVENTORY

DESCRIPTION

In this exercise you will utilize Smart Data Manager's abilities to create a database inventory for a used car lot.

A formula will be entered into the database which will calculate the profit involved in the sale of each car. Running totals will be maintained for the purchase prices, sales prices and profits.

A customized screen will be designed and the drawing of boxes and lines will be detailed.

The entering of data will be explored in depth, as well as the updating, deleting and purging of a record.

You will also scan a record using the BROWSE command, go to a record using the GOTO command and extract particular information from the database by using the FIND command.

Printing a record, selected fields, and a record in list format will be demonstrated.

OPERATIONS PERFORMED

Creating And Defining A File Structure

Defining A Record Structure

Entering A Formula Into A Database

Creating A Customized Screen And Defining Field Attributes

Drawing Boxes And Lines

Entering Data

Updating Records

Deleting A Record

Purging A File

BROWSEing Through The Records

Going To A Record (GOTO command)

FINDing A Record

Viewing The File Specifications

Printing A Record

Printing Selected Fields

Printing a Record in List Format

COMMANDS

BROWSE
CREATE
DELETE
ENTER
FILE-SPECS
FIND
GOTO
LOAD
PRINT
SAVE
UNLOAD
UPDATE
UTILITIES

CREATING AND DEFINING A FILE STRUCTURE

When Smart Data Manager is first loaded onto your screen,
Command List 1 is displayed. Press:

C	starts CREATE command
F	selects File option
autosdb	filename (**autos data base**)
RETURN	displays options
V	selects Variable-Length option
P	selects Password option

You may type any four letters you wish as a password.
However, in this exercise, type:

tree	password
RETURN	displays options
N	selects New option and displays File definition screen

DEFINING A RECORD STRUCTURE

The file structure has been defined; next you will define
the record structure.

The cursor is in the Title column. Leave the cursor where it
is and type:

Year	title of first field
RETURN	moves cursor to Type column

Observe that, in the Fld No column, the number 1 is automatically displayed, indicating that the title you just entered, Year, is the first field of your database.

Type:

A	indicates Alpha type Note: Since the years you will be entering will be considered as text, and not numbers, Alpha is the appropriate choice here.

The cursor has now moved to the Length column.

Since the years you will be entering will always consist of 4 digits, type:

4	Length
RETURN	moves cursor back to Title column

Type:

Make	title of second field
RETURN	moves cursor to Type column

Observe that the number 2 is automatically displayed underneath the number 1 in the Fld No column.

Type:

A	indicates Alpha type
20	Length
RETURN	moves cursor back to Title column

Type:

Miles	title of third field
RETURN	moves cursor to Type column

A	indicates Alpha type
	Note: Even though the miles will be entered as numbers, there will be no calculations taking place, so Alpha is appropriate here.

6	Length
RETURN	moves cursor to Title column

Type:

Description	title of fourth field
RETURN	moves cursor to Type column
A	indicates Alpha type
40	Length
RETURN	moves cursor to Title column

Type:

Purchase Date	title of fifth field
RETURN	moves cursor to Type column
D	indicates Date type

The number 8 is automatically displayed in the Length column, and the cursor has moved on to the next Title column for the next field. Type:

PPrice	title of sixth field (stands for Purchase Price)
RETURN	moves cursor to Type column
N	indicates Numeric type and displays following prompt at bottom of screen: Enter numeric precision (0-8)

For this database, it will not be necessary to allow for decimal places, so type:

0   zero decimal places

Observe that, in the Type column, N0 is displayed, meaning that the values to be entered will be Numeric and have zero decimal places.

The cursor has moved to Length column and 2 automatically displayed.

This length has to be changed.

Leave the cursor where it is, on the number 2 in the Length column, and type:

5   Length

RETURN   moves cursor to Running Total
                           column

An N has been automatically displayed in the Running Total column and the following message is now displayed at the bottom of your screen:

        Keep running total of this field (y/n)

Type:

Y   indicates Yes, keep a running total
                           of this field

Now a Y is displayed in the Running Total column, and the cursor has moved back to the Title column. Type:

Date Sold   title of seventh field

RETURN   moves cursor to Type column

D   indicates Date type

The number 8 is automatically displayed in the Length
column, and the cursor has moved on to the next Title
column for the next field. Type:

SPrice   title of eighth field
                                (stands for Selling Price)

RETURN   moves cursor to Type column

N   Numeric type

At the bottom of your screen the following prompt is
displayed:

      Enter numeric precision (0-8)

For this database, it will not be necessary to allow for
decimal places, so type:

0   zero decimal places

Observe that, in the Type column, N0 is displayed, meaning
that the values to be entered will be numeric and make no
allowance for decimal places. The cursor has moved to
Length column; 2 is automatically displayed.

This length has to be changed.

Leave the cursor where it is, on the number 2 in the Length
column, and type:

5   length

RETURN   moves cursor to Running Total column

An N has been automatically displayed in the Running Total
column and the following message is now displayed at the
bottom of your screen:

      Keep running total of this field (y/n)

Type:

Y   indicates Yes, keep a running total
                               of this field

Now a Y is displayed in the Running Total column, and the
cursor has moved back to the Title column. Type:

Profit   title of ninth field

RETURN   moves cursor to Type column

N   Numeric type

At the bottom of your screen the following prompt is
displayed:

     Enter numeric precision (0-8)

For this database, it will not be necessary to allow for
decimal places, so type:

0   zero decimal places

Observe that, in the Type column, N0 is displayed, meaning
that the values to be entered will be numeric and have no
allowance for decimal places. The cursor has moved to
Length column and 2 is automatically displayed.

This length has to be changed.

Leave the cursor where it is, on the number 2 in the Length
column, and type:

6   length

RETURN   moves cursor to Running Total
                               column

An N has been automatically displayed in the Running Total
column and the following message is now displayed at the
bottom of your screen:

     Keep running total of this field (y/n)

Y   indicates Yes, keep a running total
                                    of this field

Now a Y is displayed in the Running Total column, and the
cursor has moved back to the Title column.

ENTERING A FORMULA INTO A DATABASE

The next step is to enter a formula into the Profit field,
which will calculate the profit. This formula will subtract
the PPrice (purchase price) from the SPrice (selling price) to
calculate the profit.

Press the up arrow cursor key once, so that the cursor is on
the Profit field, and press:

F3 function key   displays Formula Editor
                                    screen

Type:

[SPrice]   Selling Price
                                    Note: the name of the field must
                                    be enclosed in brackets

-                                   minus

[PPrice]   Purchase Price

Press:

F10 function key   exits Formula Editor and
                                    displays Definition screen again

Observe that the 9th field, Profit, in the Type column, there is a C displayed after N0. The C means the field is now a Calculated field.

F10 function key   displays:
                             Are you finished defining the
                             file (y/n)

Y   Yes, saves the file

After the file is saved, the prompt: Do you want to define a key field (y/n) is displayed. Type:

N   No

Command List 1 is now displayed on your screen.

CREATING A CUSTOMIZED SCREEN AND DEFINING FIELD ATTRIBUTES

Smart Data Manager allows you to design a screen for displaying all the fields to your particular needs and taste. You will now custom design your screen and also define field attributes. The customized screen is illustrated in Figure 1. Press:

C   starts CREATE command

S   selects Screen option

Type:

Auto__Screen__1   filename of screen

RETURN   displays options

N   selects No-Password option

N   selects New option

You now have a blank screen on which you can design your database.

Year
Miles
Make
Purchase Date
FPrice
Date Sold
SPrice
Profit
NOTE: DATA WILL NOT BE ENTERED INTO THE PROFIT FIELD

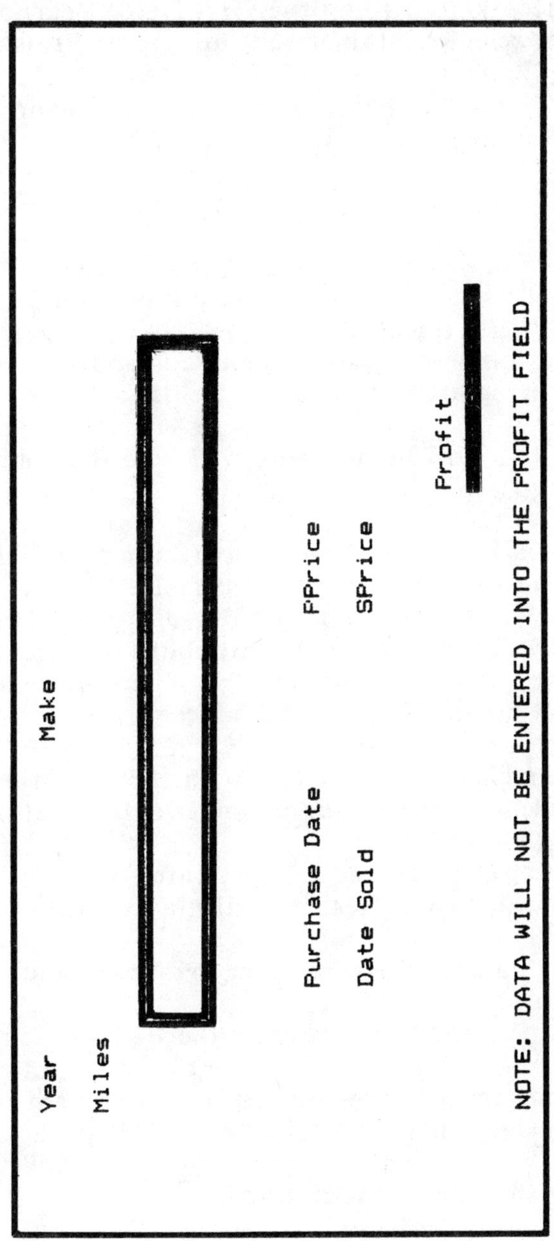

Figure 1

The first step is to display the first field, Year, on the screen, at a selected position on the screen. Press:

Tab   Tab key, moves cursor over 1 Tab
                                       position

Press:

F7 function key   displays first field, Year,
                                       at the tab position

During the course of designing the customized screen, you will also define attributes to the fields.

Attributes you will be defining will be either "must enter" or "read only".

When you define a "must enter" attribute to a field, it means that *data must be entered* into that field.

When you define a "read only" attribute to a field, it means that *no data can be entered* into that field; however, the field will be still be displayed on the screen.

For this exercise, all the fields, with the exception of the Profit field, will be defined as "must enter" fields.

The next step is to define a "must enter" attribute for the Year field, which has just been displayed on the screen.

Leave your cursor where it is, on the Year field.

Hold down the Alt key and press the F7 function key twice.

Observe that an **m** is now displayed to the right of the word Year, meaning it is now a "must enter" field.

To display the second field, press:

Tab Tab Tab   moves cursor over 3 Tab positions

F7 function key   displays second field at
                                       cursor position

Leave your cursor where it is, and hold down the Alt key
and press the F7 function key twice.

Observe that an **m** is now displayed to the right of the word
Make, meaning it is now a "must enter" field.

Press the down arrow cursor key twice.

Hold down the Shift key and press Tab until the cursor is
lined up underneath the Y in Year. Press:

F7 function key   displays third field at
                                cursor position

Leave your cursor where it is, and hold down the Alt key
and press the F7 function key twice.

Observe that an **m** is now displayed to the right of the word
Miles, meaning it is now a "must enter" field.

Press the down arrow cursor key three times. Press:

Tab   moves cursor to right one Tab
                                position

This time you will press:

F3 function key   displays fourth field, the
                                Description field, WITHOUT its
                                title

NOTE

To display a field *with* its title, press F7 function key.

To display a field *without* its title, press F3 function
key.

Leave your cursor where it is, and hold down the Alt key
and press the F7 function key twice.

Observe that an **m** is now displayed at the beginning of the
dashed line, meaning that the Description field is now a
"must enter" field.

Press the down arrow cursor key 5 times, and press:

F7 function key   displays fifth field

Leave your cursor where it is, and hold down the Alt key
and press the F7 function key twice.

Observe that an **m** is now displayed to the right of the words
Purchase Date, meaning it is now a "must enter" field.

Press the Tab key three times, and then press:

F7 function key   displays sixth field

Leave your cursor where it is, and hold down the Alt key
and press the F7 function key twice.

Observe that an **m** is now displayed to the right of PPrice,
meaning it is now a "must enter" field.

Press the down arrow cursor key twice.

Hold down the Shift key and press Tab until the cursor is
lined up underneath the P in Purchase Date, and then press:

F7 function key   displays seventh field

Leave your cursor where it is, and hold down the Alt key
and press the F7 function key twice.

Observe that an **m** is now displayed to the right of the words
Date Sold, meaning it is now a "must enter" field.

Press the Tab key three times, and then press:

F7 function key   displays eighth field

Leave your cursor where it is, and hold down the Alt key
and press the F7 function key twice.

Observe that an **m** is now displayed to the right of SPrice,
meaning it is now a "must enter" field.

Now press the down arrow cursor key 3 times, and then press
Tab once. Press:

F7 function key   displays ninth field

The message: **All fields defined** is displayed at bottom of
screen.

Hold down the Alt key and press F7 ONLY ONCE this time.

An **r** is displayed to the right of Profit, meaning that this is
now a "read only" field and, although data will be displayed,
no data can be entered here.

You decide to enter a note to that effect, so press the down
arrow cursor key 3 times.

Using Shift Tab, move the cursor to the left so that it is
lined up under the Miles field.

Press the Caps Lock key and type:

NOTE: DATA WILL NOT BE ENTERED INTO THE
PROFIT FIELD.

Press the Caps Lock key to turn it off.

DRAWING BOXES AND LINES

Smart Data Manager allows for the drawing of boxes and
lines on the customized screen.

The first art work to be performed is to draw a box around
the Description field, for added emphasis.

Place your cursor on the blank line, above the **m**, in the untitled Description field. Press the left arrow cursor key twice.

The cursor is now at the position which will be the upper left hand corner of the box which is being created.

Press:

F4 function key   displays instructions at
                                 bottom of screen

Move cursor to the blank line below the dashed line. Keep the cursor on the blank line, and position the cursor two spaces to the right of the last dash.

The cursor is now at the position which will be the lower right hand corner of the box which is being created.

Press:

RETURN   draws a double-lined box
                        around the description field

Now you want to underline the Profit field to emphasize it.

Position the cursor directly underneath the P in Profit, on the blank line, and press:

F4 function key   displays instructions at
                                 bottom of screen

Move the cursor so that it is directly underneath the last dash, and press:

RETURN   displays a double line under
                        Profit

Your screen should now look like Figure 1.

F10 function key   displays:
                        Are you through defining this
                        screen (y/n)

Y   Yes

The program now saves the custom screen.

Command list 1 is now displayed, and the fields are
displayed in column format at the top of the screen.

ENTERING DATA

To use your custom screen for entering data into the
database, you must now load it back onto the screen. Press:

4   displays Command List 4

L   starts LOAD command

autosdb   filename

RETURN   displays: Screens for file autosdb

Press the right arrow cursor key once, so that the arrow
indicator is pointing to **Autos_Screen_1**, and press:

RETURN   loads customized screen onto
                               the screen, and displays Command List 4

Press:

1   displays Command List 1

E   starts ENTER command and displays
                               customized screen with cursor at upper
                               left of screen, on the first field, Year

Observe, at the very bottom of the screen, the display:

        Page: 1 Rec: EOF (1)   Act: Y

EOF means End Of File. These letters will appear whenever
you are on the last record in the database.

The number in parenthesis is the number of the Record
which is displayed on the screen.

Act:Y means that the file is Active.

Now you are ready to make entries into Record 1 of the
database.

Leave your cursor on the Year field, and type:

1980   enters Year and automatically moves
                        cursor to next field, Make

Type:

Plymouth Horizon

To move the cursor to the next field, press:

RETURN   moves cursor to third field, Miles

Type:

42000

RETURN   moves cursor to fourth field,
                        Description

Type:

Broken door handle

RETURN   moves cursor to fifth field,
                        Purchase Date

Type:

010184   enters date and moves cursor
                                automatically to sixth field, PPrice
                                Note: It is not necessary to type the
                                hyphens in the date. Just type the
                                numbers for the date (010184).

Type:

1900

RETURN   enters purchase price and moves
                                cursor to seventh field, Date Sold

Type:

052084   enters date and moves cursor to
                                eighth field, SPrice

Type:

2400   selling price

RETURN   enters selling price and displays
                                Record 2 on your screen

NOTE

Because you earlier specified the ninth field, Profit,
to be a "read only" field, the program ignored that
field.

However, we are going back to Record 1 in order to see how
the formula in the Profit field calculated the profit for that
record. Press:

Esc   displays Record 1 and
                                Command List 1

Observe that the Profit field, because of the formula
previously entered there, now displays the Profit (500) for
that particular record. Press:

E   starts ENTER command

Record 2 (blank) is now displayed again, and you are ready
to enter data into it.

Enter the data into Records 2 and 3, as illustrated below,
pressing RETURN only where indicated.

1973
Chevrolet Camero   [RETURN]
100000
Good condition [RETURN]   (Record 2)
050284
2400 [RETURN]
061584
2600 [RETURN]

1979
Ford Mustang [RETURN]
60000 [RETURN]
Small dent in right door and scratches [RETURN]
110583
2700 [RETURN]   (Record 3)
020284
3500 [RETURN]

Blank Record 4 is now displayed on your screen.

You will now utilize Smart Data Manager's repeat ability to enter the data for the Year field.

The cursor is now on the Year field (in blank Record 4).

The year to be entered (1979) is the same as the year in Record 3.

To copy the previous Year data (1979) into Record 4, just press:

F9 function key   enters data (1979) from
                                previous record

NOTE

Anytime you wish to repeat data from a previous field, just press F9 function key.

Data will be copied from the same field of the previous record to the field you are currently on.

Press:

RETURN   moves cursor to second field, Make

Now continue entering the rest of the data for Record 4 by typing,

Chevy Luv [RETURN]
45000 [RETURN]
Faulty electric fuel line [RETURN]
012184   (Record 4)
1800 [RETURN]
021584
2300 [RETURN]

Now enter the data for Records 5, 6, 7, 8, and 9, as illustrated below.

```
1980
Chevy Luv [RETURN]
3000  [RETURN]
Bad brakes  [RETURN]                (Record 5)
040184
1400  [RETURN]
092584
1600  [RETURN]
```

NOTE

When entering the following records, don't forget to press RETURN where necessary.

```
1981
Toyota SR-5
53000
Good condition                      (Record 6)
070381
5900
110582
3300
```

```
1976
Pontiac Firebird
73000
Cracked block                       (Record 7)
012782
4000
011583
5000
```

1979
Lotus Elan
83000
Needs valve job   (Record 8)
032782
9300
070182
11000

1984
Ford Escort
21000
Good condition   (Record 9)
120884
10000
020285
11000

Blank Record 10 is now displayed on the screen. The records
are all typed in, so press:

F10 function key   exits the ENTER command and
                            displays Command List 1

UPDATING RECORDS

The Update command is used for changing data in records.
It cannot be used for adding new records.

You are now going to change some of the data in some of
the records.

The first record in which you will change data is Record 3.
Press:

U   starts UPDATE command and displays
                            at bottom of screen: UPDATE - allows
                            editing of the current record

To access Record 3, press the F5 function key until, by watching the Record number display at the bottom of the screen, you see **Page: 1 Rec: 3 (3)** displayed.

Press the F4 function key three times, so that your cursor is on the fourth field, the unlabelled Description field, and press:

F7 function key   deletes entire contents
                                     of Description field

Type:

Good condition

Next you will change some data in Record 2. Press:

F5 function key   moves backward to Record 2

Press the F4 function key five times; your cursor is now on the PPrice field. Press:

F7 function key   deletes contents of field

Type:

2500   new Purchase Price amount

The amount in Profit field remains 200. The formula in the Profit field must be recalculated. Press:

F6 function key   goes forward to Record 3

F5 function key   goes back to Record 2

Observe that the Profit field in Record 2 has now been recalculated, and the correct amount, 100, is displayed in the Profit field.

You have finished updating the records.

To exit the update, press:

F10 function key   displays Command List 1

DELETING A RECORD

A decision has been to completely delete Record 8.

First you must access the record.

Command List 1 is displayed at the bottom of the screen.
Press:

G   starts GOTO command

R   selects Record option

R   selects Rec-Number

8   Record number to go to

RETURN   displays Record 8 on the screen

To delete the record, press:

D   starts DELETE command and marks
                          the record for deletion

Observe at bottom of screen, to the far right, Act: N. This
means the record is now Not active.

PURGING A FILE

Next the file must be PURGED and the record actually
deleted from the file. To do this, you must first UNLOAD
the file. Press:

4   displays Command List 4

U   starts UNLOAD command

F   selects File option and displays,
                                 at bottom of screen, an arrow indicator
                                 pointing to the file name, **autosdb**

RETURN   unloads autosdb file

You will now use the Utilities command to purge the file.

Press:

2   displays Command list 2

U   starts UTILITIES command

P   selects Purge option

The arrow indicator is pointing to the filename: **autosdb**.

Press:

RETURN   displays message:
                                 Do you have a backup of this file y/n)

For important data, always be sure you make a backup file.

If you already have a backup file, press:

Y   Yes

The program now purges the file and permanently deletes
Record 8 from the database file.

Now load the Auto_Screen_1 back onto the screen. Press:

4   displays Command List 4

L   starts LOAD command

The arrow indicator is pointing to **autosdb**. Press:

RETURN   displays Screens for file autosdb

Press the right arrow cursor key once, so that the arrow
indicator is pointing to **Auto_Screen_1**, and press:

RETURN   loads Record 1 of the database onto
                        the screen

BROWSEing THROUGH THE RECORDS

To scan (BROWSE) the Make and the Miles fields in the
database, in order to review the models of cars, and their
mileages, press:

1   displays Command List 1

B   starts BROWSE command

F   selects Fields option

Press the right arrow cursor key once so that the arrow
indicator is pointing to the second field, **Make**, and press:

F6 function key   displays 2;

Press the right arrow cursor key once so that the arrow
indicator is pointing to the third field, Miles, and press:

F6 function key   displays 2;3;

RETURN   displays the two selected fields on
                       the screen, with all the data that was
                       entered for those fields

Your screen should look like Figure 2 below:

Make	Miles
Plymouth Horizon	**42000**
Chevrolet Camero	**100000**
Ford Mustang	**60000**
Chevy Luv	**45000**
Chevy Luv	**3000**
Toyota SR-5	**53000**
Pontiac Firebird	**73000**
Ford Escort	**21000**

Figure 2

To view the Toyota SR-5 record, in its entirety,

Press the down arrow cursor key 5 times, so that the arrow indicator is pointing to Toyota SR-5, and press:

B	selects BROWSE command and displays options
O	selects Off option

The record selected is now displayed in full screen mode.

GOING TO A RECORD (GOTO COMMAND)

The GOTO command is used to quickly go to any record in the database.

To go to Record 1 quickly, press:

G	starts GOTO command
R	selects Record option
R	selects Rec-Number option and displays: Enter record number to display:
1	record number to go to
RETURN	displays record 1

NOTE

In the database created in this exercise, there are only a few records to BROWSE through or to GOTO. However, in lengthy databases, you will appreciate Smart Data Manager's ability to rapidly access records.

FINDing A RECORD

This command allows you to specify particular information to be found, and then, by using the FIND command, extract that data.

For example, to find all records which have cars in "good condition". Press:

F   starts FIND command and displays
                            Available Fields

Press the down cursor key once so that the arrow indicator is pointing to the 4th field, Description. Press:

F6 function key   displays [4;

RETURN   displays options

E   selects Equal option

Type:

good condition

RETURN   displays options:
                Note: the options available are at the
                very bottom of the screen.

Type:

GI   (the letter **G** and the letter **I**)
                selects Global and Ignore case options

RETURN   displays Record 2, the Chevrolet
                Camero, which is in "good condition"

The message: **Data found in [Description], continue search (y/n)** is displayed.

To see if there are any more cars in good condition, press:

Y   Yes, continue search

Record 3 is displayed, the Ford Mustang, which is in "good condition".

The message: **Data found in [Description], continue search (y/n)** is displayed.

To see if there are any more cars in good condition, press:

Y   Yes, continue search

Record 6 is displayed, the Toyota SR-5, which is in "good condition".

The message: **Data found in [Description], continue search (y/n)** is displayed.

To see if there are any more cars in good condition, press:

Y   Yes, continue search

Record 8 is displayed, the Ford Escort, which is in "good . condition".

No message is displayed this time, which means there are no more cars in "good condition". Command List 1 is displayed again.

The next step is to find all cars with model years later than 1979. Press:

F   starts FIND command and displays
                                    Available fields

The arrow indicator is already pointing to **Year**, so press:

F6 function key   displays [1;

RETURN   displays options

G	selects Greater-Than option

Type:

1979

RETURN	displays options at very bottom of screen
G	selects Global option
RETURN	displays Record 1, which has a Year of 1980

Observe that this record is for a car with a date *greater than* 1979.

The message: **Data found in [Year], continue search (y/n)** is displayed.

To find the next record with a Year greater than 1979, press:

Y	Yes

Record 5 is now displayed, which has a Year of 1980.

The message: **Data found in [Year], continue search (y/n)** is displayed.

To fin the next record with a Year greater than 1979, press:

Y	Yes

Record 6 is now displayed, which has a Year of 1981.

The message: **Data found in [Year], continue search (y/n)** is displayed.

To find the next record with a Year greater than 1979, press:

Y	Yes

Record 8 is now displayed, which has a Year of 1984.

No message is displayed this time, and Command List 1 is displayed, which means there are no more records with a year greater than 1979.

VIEWING THE FILE SPECIFICATIONS

To view the running totals in the PPrice (purchase price), SPrice (selling price) and Profit fields, press:

2   displays Command List 2

F   starts FILE-SPECS command

R   selects Running-Totals option

The screen now displays Running Total information for the Purchase Price, Selling Price, and the Profit.

Your screen should look like Figure 3.

```
   Running Total Information

   Field Number   Title              Running Total
         6         PPrice                  30200
         8         SPrice                  31700
         9         Profit                   1500
```

Figure 3

To print the running total information, make sure your printer is turned on, and press:

F2 function key   prints Running Total
                             information

To exit the Running Total Information, press:

F10 function key   displays Command List 2

PRINTING A RECORD

For this exercise you are going to print Record 7.
First you must go to Record 7. Press:

1	displays Command List 1
G	starts GOTO command
R	selects Record option
R	selects Rec-Number option
7	record number to display
RETURN	displays Record 7

You are ready to print the record. Press:

P	starts PRINT command
R	selects Record option
S	selects Screen option
A	selects All option

The printer prints Record 7.

The printout should look like Figure 4.

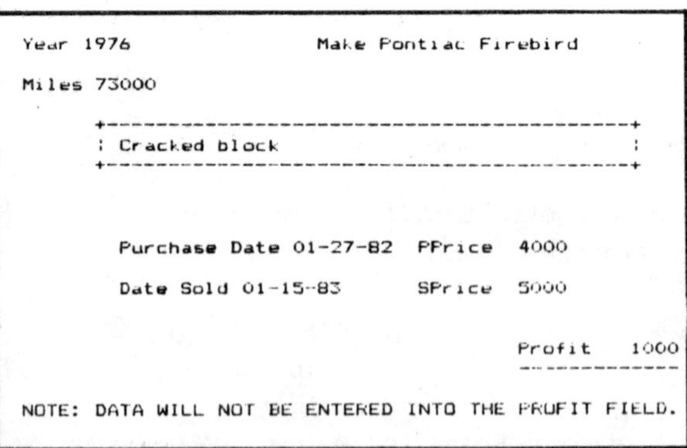

Figure 4

PRINTING SELECTED FIELDS

To print only the Year, Make and Profit fields on all the
Records, press:

P   starts PRINT comamnd

F   selects File option

R   selects Report option

You will now select the Year, Make and Profit fields for
printing to the screen.

The arrow indicator is already on Year, so press:

F6 function key

Press the right arrow cursor key once so that the arrow
indicator is pointing to Make, and press:

F6 function key

Using the arrow cursor keys, position the arrow indicator to
the left of the 9th field, Profit, and press:

F6 function key

RETURN   ends the selection and displays
                          options

P   selects Printer option, and prints

Your printout should look like Figure 5.

```
Year Make                    Profit
------------------------------------
1980 Plymouth Horizon           500
1973 Chevrolet Camero           100
1979 Ford Mustang               800
1979 Chevy Luv                  500
1980 Chevy Luv                  200
1981 Toyota SR-5              -2600
1976 Pontiac Firebird          1000
1984 Ford Escort               1000
```

Figure 5

Observe that the Toyota SR-5 shows a -2600 (minus 2600), which indicates a loss instead of a profit on that car.

PRINTING A RECORD IN LIST FORMAT

To print Record 7 in a list format, press:

P   starts PRINT command

R   selects Record option

L   selects List option, and prints

Your printout should look like Figure 6.

```
Records #: 7   Act: Y
Year: 1976
Make: Pontiac Firebird
Miles: 73000
Description: Cracked block
Purchase Date: 01-27-82
PPrice: 4000
Date Sold: 01-15-83
SPrice: 5000
Profit: 1000
```

Figure 6

DATABASE INDEX

COMMANDS AND OPERATIONS PERFORMED

COMMANDS

OPERATIONS PERFORMED

SPREADSHEET INDEX

FUNCTIONS, COMMANDS AND

OPERATIONS PERFORMED

WORD PROCESSING INDEX

COMMANDS AND OPERATIONS PERFORMED

COMMANDS

OPERATIONS PERFORMED

ORDER FORM   1·800·MANUALS

MAIL TO:
Management Information Source, Inc.
1107 N.W. 14th Avenue
Portland, Oregon 97209
(503) 222-2399

PLEASE CHARGE
☐ VISA   ☐ American Express
☐ MasterCharge   ☐ Check Enclosed

Exp. Date ___________________________

Acct. No. ___________________________

Signature ___________________________

Attn:___________________________

Company Name ___________________________

Address ___________________________

City ___________________________

State/Zip ___________________________

Phone ___________________________

Customer P.O.# ___________________________

Quantity	The following books are available	Retail Cost	Unit Cost	Discount	Total Cost
	THE MANUAL: Lotus 1-2-3	$14.95			
	THE MANUAL: Symphony	$14.95			
	THE MANUAL: Frame Work	$14.95			
	THE MANUAL: dBase II	$14.95			
	THE MANUAL: dBase III	$14.95			
	THE MANUAL: Multiplan	$14.95			
	THE MANUAL: Wordstar	$14.95			
	THE MANUAL: Apple Works	$14.95			
	THE MANUAL: Jazz	$14.95			
	THE MANUAL: Excel	$14.95			
	The Power Of: Multiplan	$14.95			
	The Power Of: Multiplan with diskette*	$28.95			
	The Power Of: Lotus 1-2-3	$14.95			
	The Power Of: Lotus 1-2-3 with diskette*	$28.95			
	The Power Of: Financial Calculations for Multiplan	$14.95			
	The Power Of: Financial Calculations for Multiplan with diskette*	$28.95			
	The Power Of: Financial Calculations for Lotus 1-2-3	$14.95			
	The Power Of: Financial Calculations for Lotus 1-2-3 with diskette*	$28.95			
	The Power Of: Construction Management Using Lotus 1-2-3	$29.95			
	The Power Of: Construction Management Using Lotus 1-2-3 with diskette*	$44.95			
	The Power Of: Construction Management Using Multiplan	$29.95			
	The Power Of: Construction Management Using Multiplan with diskette*	$44.95			
	The Power Of: The Smart Software System	$14.95			
	The Power Of: The Smart Software System with diskette*	$29.95			
	The Power Of: Microsoft Word	$14.95			
	The Power Of: Microsoft Word with diskette*	$29.95			
	The Power Of: Symphony	$14.95			
	The Power Of: Symphony with diskette*	$29.95			
	The Power Of: Framework	$14.95			
	The Power Of: Appleworks	$19.95			
	The Power Of: Appleworks with diskette (Apple-DOS)	$34.95			
	The Power Of: Visicalc, Vol. I & Vol. II	$ 9.95			
	The Power Of: Visicalc Real Estate	$14.95			
	The Power Of: SuperCalc	$ 9.95			
	The Power Of: Step By Step Through Logo Turtle Graphics	$ 6.95			
	Captain Computer & Micro Mouse Comic Coloring Book	$ 1.95			
	Video Tape of Lotus 1-2-3 Advanced Concepts	$99.95			
	Computer Top for Compaq and IBM PC	$29.95			

Shipping & Handling Charges
1 .... $1.00 per book
5-19 .... $ .35 per book
20-29 .... $ .30 per book
100 & over .... $ .15 per book

Sub Total ___________________________

Shipping & Handling ___________________________

TOTAL PRICE ___________________________

To save C.O.D. charges:
Enclose a check or use one of the above major credit cards.
Your order will be shipped U.P.S., C.O.D. within 24 hours of receipt of your order.

*MS-DOS or IBM Diskette.   Prices effective Aug. 1, 1985.